Redeeming Our Communities

Redeeming Our Communities

Twenty-first-century Miracles of Social Transformation

Debra Green

New Wine Ministries

New Wine Ministries
PO Box 17
Chichester
West Sussex
United Kingdom
PO19 2AW

Scripture quotations are taken from The Holy Bible, New International
Version. Copyright © 1973, 1978, 1984 by International Bible Society.
Used by permission of Hodder and Stoughton Limited.

ISBN 978-1-905991-09-9

Typeset by CRB Associates, Reepham, Norfolk
Cover design by CCD, www.ccdgroup.co.uk
Printed in Malta

Dedication

To Ken and Mary.
Parents are a gift from the Lord.

Contents

Acknowledgements

I would like to thank the many people and organisations who have contributed to this book by allowing us to tell their story. There are too many to list here, but you will read about them in the pages that follow.

Pete Greig has kindly written the foreword, which alone is worth buying the book for, and I am so grateful to him. His friendship over many years is precious.

Thank you to my family for being patient and understanding during the six months of writing.

Thanks to friends and fellow leaders at my church, Ivy Cottage Church in Didsbury, Manchester, for supporting me in my wider ministry.

Thanks to the City Links trustees: Robert Varnam, Rob Cannon, Andy Prosser, Julie Beemer and Julia Robertson, and the steering group of Redeeming Our Communities: Malcolm Duncan, Jane Holloway, Kevin Borg, Matt Baggott, David Muir, Frank Green, Colin Hardicre and Nick Cuthbert.

Thanks to the City Links intercessors' team whose support and prayers have been invaluable.

There are a few people worthy of particular appreciation, friends who have helped to write, research and edit this book: Jane Holloway, Catherine Proudman, Lucy Derges, Margaret Yuill and Rebekah Evans.

Special thanks to my husband, Frank, who is great with words and has added a touch of magic to some of my ordinary sentences.

What Others Are Saying About
Redeeming Our Communities

"Everyone wants to see crime falling and communities prosper, but doing so can appear a daunting challenge. It is, however, far from impossible. The *Redeeming Our Communities* story shows that the coming together of good policing, practical work by churches and focused prayer does change lives for ever."
Matt Baggott CBE – *Chief Constable, Leicestershire Constabulary*

"The Evangelical Alliance is pleased to lend its support to this important initiative. *Redeeming Our Communities* is a prophetic and practical way to demonstrate Christian commitment to work for safe, prosperous and peaceful communities. It is community cohesion at its best. By working with the Police, churches and key criminal justice and education partners this initiative tries to fulfil the mandate of Jeremiah 29:7: to seek and pray for the peace and prosperity of our communities."
Dr R. David Muir – *Director of Public Policy, Evangelical Alliance*

"Debra has displayed a unique tenacity in following her divine destiny through the trying times of initial organisation up to the present and remarkable fulfilment of God's revelation. From small beginnings, this prayer and transformation ministry has flourished in ways that can only be called miraculous and has real statistical proof of the power of prayer to affect local communities and indeed nations. She stands out as an inspiration to her generation and living proof that God answers the prayers of his saints especially when they pray for prayer."

Bishop (Dr) Doyé Agama – *Chair of the Apostolic Pastoral Association and Black & Minority Ethnic Christian Association*

"It's been thrilling to watch churches across the UK get even more engaged in their local communities over the last few years. Debra's work and this timely book are playing a key part in fuelling this God-given vision."

Andy Hawthorne – *CEO, The Message Trust*

"Debra's passion for people, faith in God and quest for justice are inspiring. Her work is fantastic and this book is a must read for anyone who wants to see their communities become safer places."

Malcolm Duncan – *Leader of Faithworks*

"I have long believed that prayer + action leads to transformation – not just of individuals, but of communities as well. My hope is that this book will encourage us to continue to pray and work until we see the causes of crime removed and crime reduced."

Jane Holloway – *National Prayer Director, World Prayer Centre, Birmingham*

Foreword

A few years ago, I spotted a Christmas card depicting a typical English town centre frosted with snow. Sparkling shops were lining the High Street and crowds of Christmas shoppers, with breath like steam, were bustling between stores. Above them a large, festive banner stretched the breadth of the High Street saying: "GLORY IN THE HIGHEST". However, some wise-card had crossed out the "E" in "HIGHEST" so that the banner now simply read: "GLORY IN THE HIGH ST".

This new book from Debra Green earths the glorious story of Christ's birth, life, death and resurrection in "The High Street", which is to say that it relates to the real world of shops, offices, schools and hospitals, industry, local govern-ment and even crime-prevention. It grounds the good news of the Gospel amongst the people with whom we try to do that whole, tricky "love your neighbour" thing. It echoes the heart cry of Jesus who so loved the world that He swapped glory in the highest for birth in a cattle trough outside a busy pub and never stopped talking about this kingdom of heaven which can transform people, places and entire communities.

We look back at Jesus and then we look around us at the problems of modern society, despairing in our darker moments at the apparent irrelevance of His Church, and we may secretly wonder if it is still possible for communities like these to be redeemed. How on earth does the "glory of God in the highest" impact today's suburban sprawl, the rural parish or the rising gang culture? How, to frame the same question theologically, does personal salvation become social transformation? Can our prayer meetings really change the world?

Debra Green believes that our communities can be redeemed by Jesus today, just as they have been in the past. In fact, she doesn't just believe it, she *knows* it. She has *seen* it, as the stories in this book attest! Isn't this our deepest longing once we have tasted the redemption of Jesus in our own lives: to see others impacted too? To see salvation outworked dynamically in society? To hear that crime rates and un-employment rates and divorce rates are all falling? I confess that I sometimes get weary of hearing about such revivals at other times in history or in other places in the world. "Do it *here*, Lord," I say. "Do it *now* amongst *these* people, in *this* place, in *these* streets" (see Habakkuk 3:2).

Handle with care

I know Debra Green well enough to realise that the book in your hands is more than just a biblical response to one of the greatest longings of the Church at this time. It is also, in many ways, her life message. Debra Green lives to see communities redeemed and she has learned the lessons revealed in this book the hard way, day-to-day, over many years serving and praying like crazy in and for the great industrial City of Manchester. And the thrilling thing, as you will see, is that it's working! Latest statistics suggest that the Church in Manchester is growing again at last, especially amongst young people, and that communities really are being impacted, reconciled and transformed across the City. This book absolutely bubbles over with practical stories about the difference that the people of God have made through intelligent, united prayer expressed sacrificially in society.

In many ways Debra is a prophetic voice to the Church

because she is also a peacemaker in society who can broker creative relationships between statutory and spiritual authorities and across denominational divides. But she is also experienced as a local church pastor, actively engaged with the nitty-gritty daily challenges of congregational life. And underpinning her many gifts, pastoral, prophetic and peacemaking, Debra is a prayer warrior who has mobilised thousands of people to intercede with their whole lives for the coming of Christ's Kingdom "on earth as it is in heaven".

A few years ago I invited Debra to attend a conference which was to take place in Amsterdam, right on the edge of the city's infamous red light district. The delegates were all young activists in the 24-7 Prayer movement, determined to live out their faith in Jesus at the very interface between prayer, mission and justice. We had asked Debra to do a little bit of teaching, but mainly just to hang out and be available as a friend and mentor. One afternoon we invited those who felt called to plant new expressions of church to stand. I wasn't surprised when almost every person in the room immediately rose to their feet. I began praying for people at the front of the crowd, but Debra was nowhere to be seen, just when we needed her! As I ministered to people, I couldn't help noticing that heads kept disappearing from the middle and back of the crowd. They were just vanishing! One minute I'd see someone standing there serenely with their eyes closed and the next they were gone. Faces that had been clearly visible one moment were nowhere to be seen when I looked for them moments later. At last, I identified the cause. Debra (who is not the tallest person in the world) was quietly wandering through the throng, gently laying hands on people. That was when their faces would invariably vanish! They seemed to be systematically toppling to the floor wherever Debra went and whenever she prayed!

That little snapshot from Amsterdam conveys so many of the things I appreciate about Debra. She was right in the thick of the people, quietly and dangerously impacting lives. She was also modelling the connection between our passion for change and her understanding of the power of prayer, recognising that practical and spiritual dynamics must intersect. Debra, who had been happy to fly to Amsterdam simply to be a friend, was busily encouraging, affirming and exhorting us, and she was doing it right there in the broken heart of that great city.

Injecting Jesus

God's servants have always understood the relationship between the redemption of individuals and the transformation of entire communities. On Christmas Day, 1977, Archbishop Oscar Romero stood in his pulpit in San Salvador to preach. "With Christ," he said, "God has injected himself into history. With the birth of Christ, God's reign is now inaugurated into human time." Romero knew that Christ's birth, heralded by angels singing "Glory in the highest", had practical, social, economic and political implications in the making of history. God injects himself – what a memorable phrase! – into the veins of this sick body. Archbishop Romero preached courageously against the systems oppressing the poor of his nation, because he believed that the hope of every community is only, ultimately Christ. The powers wanted a Church (and indeed an Archbishop) in San Salvador that would deal with a narrow set of "spiritual" irrelevancies. The powers did not want the Church to meddle in the "worldly" business of government. Those powers would eventually shoot Romero dead with a single bullet to the heart during a Mass in 1980. His blood, it is said, spilled across the altar and even into the communion wine.

By the blood of Jesus we are saved. And having redeemed us He calls us, as the community of the redeemed, to redeem the very communities of which we are a part. I am delighted to commend a book like Debra's which exhorts, equips and encourages us to do exactly this.

Oscar Romero finished his Christmas homily that day with a reminder that our communities can be redeemed, not because we are clever, determined or powerful, but simply, astonishingly, because Jesus Christ lives, dies and rises again amongst us. He is born here in these streets. He cries and He dies here. May He rise amongst us too. That Christmas card was right: His glory – the glory of the heavens – really has come to the High Street.

> "Humans long for peace, for justice, for a reign of divine law, for something holy, for what is far from earth's realities. We can have such a hope, not because we ourselves are able to construct the realm of happiness that God's holy words proclaim, but because the builder of a reign of justice, of love, and of peace is already in the midst of us."[1]

Pete Greig
Guildford, England
www.24-7prayer.com

Notes

1. Oscar Romero, *The Violence of Love*, tr. James R. Brockman (New York: Orbis Books, 1988), p. 25.

Introduction

Common goals

When I heard a cabinet minister say, "I believe in community redemption – I have to, I'm a politician," I felt as though someone had plugged me in to an electrical socket. Redemption was not a word you normally came across in secular circles, but I'd been hearing it more and more lately on the lips of Police chiefs, senior city council executives, and spotting it frequently in government reports. They were speaking our language!

It was September 2004 and we had just launched our latest initiative, *Redeeming Our Communities* (ROC), aimed at building on the amazing experiences of Festival:Manchester (see Chapter 6 for details). The idea was to keep the partnerships going between churches, Police and local authorities that had proved so effective during the recent citywide mission. It had been thrilling to see secular agencies working alongside Christian groups with enthusiasm and mutual respect, all sharing a common heart and vision – to see local communities transformed. It had worked well in Manchester and we felt God was calling us to challenge the North West to follow suit.

Over 1,000 people turned up to the event in the conference centre of Bolton Wanderers' Reebok Stadium, including Chief Executives from various city councils, high-ranking Police officers from a number of different forces and MPs from across the North-West. Many of these were not even churchgoers, let alone committed Christians, and yet the sense of shared vision was clear. Hazel Blears gave an impassioned address calling for more of the kind of co-operation we'd seen over the last year or so and the Bishop of Bolton prayed for more of God's power to enable everyone to deliver. The phrase, "singing from the same hymn sheet", had never seemed more appropriate. We cheered as Police chiefs fed back figures that showed dramatic drops in crime in the specific areas we'd been involved in. Everyone present went away encouraged to maintain and develop these partnerships of prayer and practical action.

Here are a few excerpts from letters and emails I received after the event:

"I was greatly impressed by the whole occasion and the various presentations and it was no less than inspirational. There was an extremely powerful message connecting religion and faith with personal responsibility and community action and with the critical role the Police play in our communities. I wish the project every success."
Robert Hough – *High Sheriff of Greater Manchester*

"What a fantastic night. We got loads of ideas for Lancashire and our church. You and your team did a great job".
Chris Gradwell – *Community Beat Manager Co-ordinator, Lancashire Police*

"We should have more evenings like this!"
Hazel Blears – *MP for Salford and Home Office Minister*

"I am always pleased to develop partnerships with those who have a long term commitment to work in and for our communities ... Together we really can make a difference and I applaud your commitment and efforts."
Michael Todd – *Chief Constable, Greater Manchester Police*

"I enjoyed the evening and subsequently I intend to ensure that Sefton plays a very positive role in *Merseyfest 2005.*"
Graham Haywood – *Chief Executive, Sefton Council, Merseyside*

"We want to send you our wholehearted encouragement as you launch this pioneering initiative of partnership between police, churches and the communities across the North West of England founded on prayer ... (hopefully it will) be a transferable model to other cities across the UK and beyond."
Evangelical Alliance – *in 2004, Malcolm Duncan (Head of Mission), Jane Holloway (Prayer & Evangelism)*[1] *Julia Wensley (Social Responsibility)*

It seemed to me that God was opening doors for the Church to demonstrate the truth of the Gospel in a new and exciting way. He seemed to be granting favour to these novel and unusual partnerships and I sensed His call to promote and enable them wherever possible. Over the following months I received invitations to help establish ROC type activities in other parts of the UK and in May 2006 we held a national launch at the NEC alongside a Trumpet Call prayer event. Over 7,000 attended, again including many MPs, Police chiefs and senior leaders from secular authorities. Once again, the common agenda to see crime fall and social conditions improve was the dominant theme and the sense of shared vision was amazing as stories of community redemption were celebrated by the unusually diverse audience.

I have been privileged to work closely with groups in dozens of towns and cities since then and excited to see the variety of approaches people are taking to meet this challenge. Each area has its own unique set of social priorities and the stories I have heard and seen are inspiring both by virtue of the creative and energetic responses to these and the frequently miraculous answers to prayer. John Wesley once declared, "God does nothing except in answer to prayer" which, in my opinion, is slightly overstating the point, but I know what he meant!

This book is intended to showcase a number of examples of how churches have co-operated with secular authorities both in Britain and in other parts of the world. I hope and pray it will play its part in the creation of many more. There is a unique window of opportunity here for the glory of God to be seen in a tangible and magnetic way. Let's grasp the chance with both hands while we can. Our communities are crying out for liberation. In the words of the renowned German theologian Karl Barth, "The [Christian] community speaks in the surrounding world by the positions it takes on the political, social and cultural problems of the world,"[2] which means it is essential that the Church and individual Christians involve themselves in current issues in order to "speak" to the surrounding world. It is up to us to channel the love, peace and justice of Jesus into the "voice" of our communities and to ensure that Christians are eagerly invited into the dialogue about community.

The agenda of Satan is evident everywhere in our society: selfishness, greed, complacency, hatred, aggression; and people are enslaved to debt, addictions, materialism and all kinds of idolatry. God is calling His people to rise up and fight back, to march together into the enemy's camp and take back (redeem) that which has been bought back (redeemed) through the work of His Son, Jesus Christ.

Notes

1. Malcolm Duncan is now Leader of Faithworks and Jane Holloway is now the National Prayer Director of The World Prayer Centre, both are members of the National Steering Group for the "Redeeming Our Communities" initiative.
2. Barth, *Evangelical Theology*, p. 40.

CHAPTER 1

A New Reformation?

Over the last few years a number of Christian writers have speculated that the time is ripe for a new Reformation that would help the Church and its teaching to become more accessible for post-modern people. They feel that current doctrines and practices are becoming increasingly irrelevant to non-churchgoers and they are concerned about the Church losing touch completely with the outside world and becoming more and more marginalised in society, even disappearing altogether.

I'm sure these New Reformers are right and I applaud them for what they are doing. We do need to make sure that the Christian faith is explained in ways that make sense to contemporary culture. And we do need to make sure that the way we "do church" is at least not a stumbling block to not-yet-Christians and at best manages to attract people to Jesus. This is the task of every generation of believers in every nation of the world.

I'm not sure, though, that this is all we need. In fact, I am sure it isn't!

The Reformation of the Church in Europe which began in the sixteenth century was mainly concerned with theology, philosophy and papal power. Huge characters like Luther, Calvin and Zwingli poured their intellectual energy into questioning doctrines which they believed were concealing the amazing truth of the Gospel from ordinary people and keeping the clergy in control. The Scriptures had recently begun to be translated into German, English and other modern languages, directly from the original Hebrew and Greek. The invention of the printing press had made these widely available, which meant that ordinary people could read them for themselves. Church services now didn't need to be conducted in Latin and Church traditions and doctrines could be examined by everybody in the light of the teaching of the Bible.

One noticeable difference between sixteenth-century Europe and the twenty-first-century global village we inhabit today is that the Church played a central role in society in those days whereas, in the main, today's general public is not particularly affected by or even in any sort of contact with the Church. The vast majority of people now don't really care whether we baptise infants or not. They don't mind whether churches are governed by Bishops or boards of Elders. Questions about whether it's possible for a Christian to lose her or his salvation are of no interest whatsoever. Even the identity of the Beast of Revelation doesn't figure in the top 100 discussion topics at a table in the average Starbucks. Ordinary people are not concerned about our churchy agenda at all. Changing our structures, renaming our activities, refocusing our regular gatherings so that every-day issues become more central, will help the *churchgoing* population to become more aware of the importance of the kingdom of God in the everyday world of work, rest and play, but the impact on the world at large will be minimal.

What's needed is not just a New Reformation that makes the Word of God more accessible, we also need a revival of faith-fuelled activism that makes the heart of God more visible.

Working to reform our churches doesn't attract the attention of a largely agnostic society, working to redeem our communities certainly does. When Christians roll up their sleeves and get stuck into social improvement, people take notice. To quote Barth again, "Theology is a service in and for the community from the tradition of the community."[1]

Tom Wright, in his inspirational book *The Challenge of Jesus*, proposes: "Our task, as image-bearing, God-loving, Christ-shaped, Spirit-filled Christians, following Christ and shaping our world, is to announce redemption to the world that has discovered its fallenness; to announce healing to the world that has discovered its brokenness; to proclaim love and trust to the world that knows only exploitation, fear and suspicion."[2]

I find it fascinating that the Reformation paved the way for an explosion of social transformation ministries over the next couple of centuries. God raised up many key Christian leaders who not only preached the truth of the Gospel with great power, but also got to grips with the social ills of their society through practical action. It wasn't enough for them to convert and disciple individuals, important as this was, they also wanted to see the power of God bring wholesale change to towns and cities where poverty, disease and injustice dominated, even to the extent of influencing the welfare of an entire nation.

Maybe it is indeed time for a New Reformation, but it's also time for new Social Reformers to emerge as well to attack *today's* expressions of evil that are eating away at the fabric of our society.

As the truth of the Gospel spread in the sixteenth and seventeenth centuries, the Western world enjoyed more and more social reform as many Christians became pioneers of societal transformation.

John Wesley

The founder of Methodism, Wesley not only covered over a quarter of a million miles on horseback to preach over forty thousand sermons (mainly in the open air to gatherings of thousands), but also visited prisons and poor houses with gifts of food, clothing and medical care, established the Stranger's Friend Society to give practical help to the poor, and was one of the earliest opponents of slavery. For him there was no need to separate the practice of good works from the preaching of the good news.

His ministry not only saw enormous numbers of people converted, but also led to massive social change in the UK. Many historians believe that it was this that prevented Britain from following the path taken by the French who turned to secular philosophy and violent revolution in an attempt to improve society.

William Wilberforce

A deeply religious English member of parliament and social reformer, Wilberforce was very influential in the abolition of the slave trade and eventually slavery itself throughout the British Empire. His Christian faith prompted him to become interested in social reform, particularly the improvement of factory conditions in Britain.

The abolitionist Thomas Clarkson had an enormous influence on Wilberforce. He and others were campaigning for an end to the trade in which British ships were carrying black slaves from Africa, in terrible conditions, to the West Indies as goods to be bought and sold. Around one hundred thousand slaves each year were being transported across the Atlantic, with, on average, a third dying on the journey. Wilberforce was persuaded to lobby for the abolition of the slave trade and for eighteen years he regularly introduced anti-slavery motions in parliament. In 1807, the slave trade was finally abolished, but this did not free those who were already slaves. It was not until 1833 that an act was passed giving freedom to all slaves in the British Empire.

Wilberforce's other efforts to "renew society" included the organisation of the Society for the Suppression of Vice in 1802. He worked with the reformer, Hannah More, in the Association for the Better Observance of Sunday. Its goal was to provide all children with regular education in reading, personal hygiene and religion. He was also closely involved with the Royal Society for the Prevention of Cruelty to Animals.

Elizabeth Fry

Born into a wealthy Quaker family in 1780, Elizabeth Fry tolerated religion for seventeen years before recording in her journal that she had ceased to believe in any kind of God. Within a year, however, she attended a Gospel meeting and was soundly converted. She immediately threw herself into many charitable works in her home city of Norwich, including making clothes for the poor and caring for destitute children. She was given a prophetic word that she would be "a light to the blind, a voice to the dumb and feet to the lame". She went on to open soup kitchens and a school and, as well as bringing up her own family, she began to visit Newgate Prison where she taught women and girls to knit and sew and helped them to sell the clothes they made to provide them with some income. Alongside this she held daily Bible readings and prayer meetings at 9 a.m. and 6 p.m. to which all the women prisoners were summoned. Her work-creation schemes were a great success and she was invited to set them up at other prisons all around the UK and even throughout Europe. She met the King of France, Louis Phillipe, and was referred to by the King of Prussia as "his friend".

As a direct result of Elizabeth's ministry, many reforms

were introduced in prisons all over the world, with the assertion that all prisoners should be treated humanely at the core. She will be mainly remembered for challenging and reforming the abuses suffered by female prisoners during transportation to Australia (a common practice in the eighteenth century even as a punishment for minor offences, such as stealing a side of bacon, which was punishable by life imprisonment, or stealing a pair of shoes, which carried a sentence of fourteen years). Women convicts were chained together and carried in open carts to the ships where they would spend the long voyage in appalling conditions with no medical attention. In the penal colony they were treated as slaves and given neither employment nor accommodation.

As a result of Fry's activism all of this changed and the women were treated with dignity and respect: they were taken to the ships in closed Hackney carriages; once aboard, their chains were removed and each one was given a Bible and a sewing and knitting kit with materials to make clothes. Major changes were made at the penal colonies. Over a period of twenty five years Elizabeth Fry personally visited twelve thousand convicted women on board ships bound for Botany Bay. Eventually, the whole practice of transportation was stopped as a result of her tireless campaigning.

William and Catherine Booth

Born in Nottingham in 1829, Booth knew the bitter taste of poverty. His father died when he was fourteen and he became a pawnbroker's apprentice. He never forgot the anxiety, the bleakness and, above all, the degradation of being poor. He would eventually startle Britain with his book, *In Darkest England and the Way Out*,[3] which told of people who worked themselves into exhaustion and then died from starvation, unable to afford as much food as the British government guaranteed the worst criminals in the nation's jails. In 1890, the year his book appeared, there were three million such people in England.

Despite the fact that it was this kind of social injustice that fuelled his ministry to the poor, Booth was never tempted to become an agent merely of social change; he was always the evangelist. Converted at age fifteen in a Wesleyan chapel, he vowed only to "declare the Word of Truth which brings Life to its hearers and sets them on the Way of discipleship". For Booth, however, evangelism could not be removed from social transformation, the two went hand in hand. Not everyone shared his view of mission though. He was soon dismissed by Church authorities as a "reformer" and was stripped of his clergy-standing.

Together with his wife, Catherine Mumford, he began conducting preaching missions in Wales, Cornwall, and the Midlands – areas that had suffered the worst economic and human blight in the shadow-side of industrialisation. In 1865 they opened the Christian Mission in East London. In 1878 it was renamed "The Salvation Army".

Persecution began immediately. "Take their flag, tie it round their necks and hang 'em," fumed the mayor of Folkestone. Following outdoor services in Sheffield in 1882, William Booth "reviewed" his stalwart soldiers. They were bespattered with egg-yolk, mud and blood, their brass instruments battered beyond repair. "Now is the time to have your photographs taken," he commented wryly. In that year alone seven hundred Salvationists were assaulted on the streets of Great Britain.

Catherine was the intellectual genius of the organisation. As highly-born as her husband was not (her father had been a clergyman), Catherine was gifted with a keen mind, unshakable conviction and resolute courage. Long periods of childhood illness had led her to probe philosophy, theology and history. She had read through the entire Bible by age twelve. She would eventually write compellingly on behalf of women preachers. Her husband agreed with her in this. The Orders and Regulations that he drafted maintained that "women should have the right to equal share with men in the work of publishing salvation". He also insisted that "women must be treated as equal with men in all intellectual and social relationships of life".

Booth continued his multi-pronged attack on the strongholds of evil. On the one hand he unashamedly instructed the evangelists he trained to "preach damnation with the cross at the centre". On the other hand he never rested until he had secured permanent changes in the world around him. He fought for the "dirt-poor, phossy-jawed" workers in the match-making industry who found their jawbones glowing in the dark and their lives at risk because of the phosphorus they were obliged to work with. Tirelessly he exposed the "white slave" trade: thirteen to sixteen year old prostitutes who were much in demand in Paris and London. Three hundred and ninety-six thousand signatures later, he saw the practice outlawed.

At his death in 1912 The Salvation Army had almost ten thousand congregations throughout the world. The organisation is now found in ninety-four countries, stretching from India, the site of the first major overseas venture, to El Salvador, added in 1989. The most recent additions are Hungary, Czechoslovakia, Latvia and Russia.

The Booths had always known that the work of God would advance only if Christians dedicated themselves without hesitation or qualification, not only to preaching the Gospel, but also to attacking social injustice. William wrote,

> While women weep, as they do now, I'll fight;
> While little children go hungry, I'll fight;
> While men go to prison, in and out, in and out, I'll fight;
> While there is a drunkard left,
> While there is a poor lost girl on the streets,

Where there remains one dark soul without the light of God
   – I'll fight!
I'll fight to the very end!

Our twenty-first-century challenge

These Social Reformers from years gone by have inspired
millions of Christians to follow in their footsteps and yet the
surface remains only slightly scratched.

Why is this? Well, one reason is that we're not really sure
where we stand biblically in terms of our understanding of the
Gospel. Many evangelical Christians have been taught that
"doing good works" is not only unnecessary, but may even be
a distraction from the really important task of preaching the
Gospel. Traditionally, "social action" has been the province of
"liberals"; those who considered themselves "true Christians"
would prioritise the need to proclaim and explain the Gospel
so that individual sinners could come to repentance and faith.

Thankfully, this dualism between the preaching and prac-
tise of the Gospel is rapidly fading into the background. Only a
tiny minority of evangelicals still cling to the old definitions.
Most, if not all of today's evangelistic organisations embrace a
more balanced and holistic view, as do most church denominations and streams. There is a new generation of believers
emerging that don't even know there's an issue! They read
verses like Mathew 25:35ff. and James 2:14ff. alongside
Matthew 28:18–20 and just get on with the job.

Another reason is certainly to do with our lack of planned
co-operation as churches and mission agencies. This is not
normally deliberate (although there are, sadly, some who
will not join forces with anyone else, sometimes because
of doctrinal differences, sometimes perhaps due to a lack of
awareness of their need of others), it's usually just the result
of busy programmes and/or a lack of opportunity. One of the
central themes of this book is unity: churches joining forces

with each other to pray about the social issues of their immediate community and then linking up with local authorities, Police and other secular groups who share a common vision. The realisation that it all starts with prayer should be a real encouragement to all of us because that's something we can all do. My experience has consistently been that when Christians start to seek God *together* in prayer about community transformation it never takes long before some ideas and plans emerge.

A third reason why we've still such a long way to go in our attempts to see society transformed is that we're often not confident in our ability to achieve anything significant. We consider the magnitude of, say, gun crime or drug abuse in our town or city and we imagine there's little, if anything, we can do about it. Back to the previous point: in prayer we have a weapon of great power. Some of the testimonies you'll be reading about in later chapters will encourage you enormously to trust God with the big challenges. Remember, He is able to do immeasurably more than we can even imagine and He cares more about the state of our communities than anyone.

God's kingdom is advancing

Fourth, and maybe this last reason is the most significant, we may not really believe that it's even God's will to redeem communities. Maybe, deep down, we believe that God will one day simply destroy everything He's made and create something new from scratch, something which is completely good and with no possibility of the existence of evil.

This is an issue to do with our view of the kingdom of God. If we believe that God's kingdom is primarily an otherworldly thing and that, although it is here in part (in some mysterious way), most of it is still to come (i.e. at the Second Coming of Jesus), then we will probably not be very motivated about working for change in the here-and-now.

A similar issue exists when we think about caring for the environment. Some of us believe that this earth is only a temporary thing – a place of preparation for us before we go to heaven. When the End comes, God will destroy this earth and replace it with a shiny new model. Therefore, what's the point of caring for creation? Why bother recycling our used materials? Why bother reducing carbon emissions? In fact, if you take this to its logical conclusion, perhaps we should help God to destroy the earth by consuming and wasting more of its resources!

What we believe certainly affects the way we live.

If, however, we believe that God is *renewing* the creation, and, although there may well be some major catastrophic purging to do at the very end, He is nevertheless going to modify and preserve the created order for all time, then we'll be more inclined to participate in the kind of redemptive activity that extends to more than just individual human beings.

Jesus spoke a great deal about the kingdom of God. In fact, there's more recorded in the Gospels on His lips relating to this than any other subject. By "kingdom" Jesus means "rule" or "influence". The kingdom of God is not a geographical location like the United Kingdom, it's a description of God's sovereignty being exercised within the creation (your kingdom come, on earth, as it is in heaven). So, the kingdom of God is God's sphere of influence. It is not confined to the heavenly realm, it has broken into the earthly sphere in the person of Jesus (Luke 11:20). The kingdom of God is among us, although clearly there is still more to come. When Jesus returns in glory the kingdom of God will come in all its fullness. Evil will be vanquished and God's perfect and irresistible rule will be established throughout the created order.

Two of Jesus' parables, found in Matthew 13, give us some really helpful insight into the nature of the kingdom. In the first one (verses 31–32), the parable of the mustard seed, the kingdom is pictured as something that starts small and grows steadily into an all-embracing entity ("The birds make their home in its branches" is a picture of this). In the second parable (verse 33), that of yeast mixed into dough, the kingdom is pictured as a force that permeates every area of the creation and influences everything with which it comes into contact. Just as yeast causes the whole batch of dough to rise, so the kingdom of God will gradually, yet totally, transform the whole of God's creation.

We are called to be God's co-workers in advancing His kingdom on the earth. Our task is not just to explain the way of salvation to individuals, but to act as agents of change in society as well. God cares that people struggle with debt in the affluent West as much as He cares about people dying of starvation in Africa. He's not only concerned about the rights and wrongs of burglary, muggings and vandalism, but also about the degrading effect that crime has on a community. As His rule advances in the world it will confront these expressions of evil and begin to reverse them. That's what redemption is – to restore something to its original state, to take back that which has been stolen, to put right that which has been spoiled. Once we understand this core meaning of the kingdom of God, it's easy to see how we should play our part.

Notes

1. Barth, *Evangelical Theology*, p. 44.
2. N.T. Wright, *The Challenge of Jesus* (London: SPCK, 2000), p. 142.
3. Updated by twenty-first-century Manchester-based Salvationist, Gary Bishop, entitled *Darkest England – and the Way Back In* (Matador Books, 2007). Gary tells compelling stories of community redemption based on his first-hand experience of working in one of the toughest inner-city areas of Manchester.

Redemption Begins at Home

I have been privileged to be involved in an amazing move of God that has begun to transform my own city of Manchester over the last decade or so. The story is told in depth and detail in a book written by myself and my husband, Frank, a few years ago: *City-Changing Prayer* (Survivor, 2005), but I want to summarise it briefly here to set the scene for the rest of this book and to add some fresh material to cover what has happened most recently on my own doorstep.

Manchester is a fascinating city with just about every kind of social problem imaginable mixed in with a vibrant music, arts, sports and fashion culture that rivals even the most famous cities of the world.

When I travel to other parts of the UK or abroad, I come across some interesting references to Manchester, most of which are stereotypical clichés. We seem to be known for lots of rainfall, Manchester United Football Club, Coronation Street, dangerous streets and gang warfare, among other things. I remember a few years ago being asked several times by concerned parents if their teenage children would be safe if they came to Manchester to work on one of our Christian Festivals.

I was born in Manchester and have lived most of my life here. My parents and their parents going back generations are

Mancunians, and all four of my children were born here. So I suppose I have a lot of reason to love Manchester, warts and all.

A recent event has brought the popular image of Manchester back into the forefront of our minds. Tony Wilson, widely regarded as the man who put Manchester on the map for its music and vibrant nightlife, died at the age of fifty-seven in August 2007. He was a broadcaster, journalist and nightclub owner who described himself as "a professional Mancunian". Tony was a founder of Factory Records in the late 1970s, the label behind Joy Division, New Order and The Happy Mondays. In 1982, he set up The Hacienda nightclub, which became known as perhaps the most famous club in the world in the late 1980s and early 1990s. I did not know Tony personally but it was very clear that he loved Manchester. On one of the tributes recorded, the story is told that he once travelled to London for an interview for a big job, but on arrival he got the train straight back to Manchester because he did not want to be anywhere else!

(Motto) *"Concilio Et Labore"* ("Wisdom and effort")

It is claimed that Manchester was the world's first industrialised city and is notable for the central role it played during the Industrial Revolution. It was the dominant international centre of textile manufacture and cotton spinning. During the nineteenth century it acquired the nickname *Cottonopolis* suggesting that the area was a metropolis of cotton mills. Manchester City centre is now on a "tentative list" of UNESCO World Heritage Sites, mainly due to the network of canals and mills that facilitated its development during the nineteenth century.

Friedrich Engels, the famous nineteenth-century German social scientist, was impressed by the spirit of the city's people during the time he spent working here in his father's factory.

It was during this time that he wrote his well-known book, *The Condition of the Working-Class in England in 1844*, which includes this quote,

> "Manchester, in South-east Lancashire, rapidly rose from obscurity to become the premier centre of cotton manufacture in England. This was largely due to geography. Its famously damp climate was better for cotton manufacture than the drier climate of the older eastern English cloth manufacture centres. It was close to the Atlantic port of Liverpool (and was eventually connected by one of the earliest rail tracks, as well as an ocean ship capable canal – although thirty miles inland, it was long a major port). It was also close to power sources – first the water power of the Pennine mountain chain, and later the coal mines of central Lancashire. As a result, Manchester became perhaps the first modern industrial city."[1]

Manchester is a city and metropolitan borough of Greater Manchester, England. The City of Manchester metropolitan borough, which has city status, has a population of 452,000. Manchester lies at the centre of the wider Greater Manchester Urban Area, which has a population of 2,240,230, the United Kingdom's third largest conurbation. It is also the second largest urban zone in the UK and the fourteenth most populated in Europe.

Although, according to the Manchester Tourist board, the population of Manchester is much higher: "The quoted population of around 400,000 is a nonsense. The city should be viewed in the same way as the city of London: a significant part of the whole. Manchester proper, the continuously built up area within the central area of the conurbation, would then give a population figure of around a million."

Forming part of the *English Core Cities Group*, and often described as the "Capital of the North", Manchester today is a centre of the arts, the media, higher education and commerce.

In a recent poll of British business leaders, Manchester was regarded as the best place to locate business in the UK. A report commissioned by Manchester Partnership, published in 2007, showed Manchester to be the "fastest-growing city" economically. It is the third most visited city in the United Kingdom by foreign visitors and is now often considered to be the second city of the UK. Manchester was the host of the 2002 Commonwealth Games and among its other sporting connections are its two Premier League football teams, Manchester City and Manchester United.

Over the last ten years or so, Manchester has experienced massive regeneration. The IRA bomb on 15th June, Fathers Day, in 1996 sparked a new wave of improvements to the city centre. Over two hundred people were injured and over 50,000 square metres of retail space destroyed, including much damage to the cathedral. In the months and years that followed much of the city centre underwent reconstruction. When Manchester won the bid to host the Commonwealth Games, another phase of regeneration began. The city now boasts many new and improved buildings and features, including the new Manchester City Stadium, now home to Manchester City Football Club.

Prepare the way

Manchester is also a pioneer city. For example:

- in 1787 Thomas Clarkson started a public campaign for the abolition of the slave trade. 11,000 inhabitants of Manchester subscribed it after he delivered a speech in Manchester Cathedral
- the first British Congress of Trade Unions was held in Manchester
- the Labour Party started in Manchester
- the women's Suffragette Movement started in Manchester

- the Anti-Corn Law League started in Manchester
- Marx and Engels worked here and wrote their most influential books in Manchester: *The Communist Manifesto* and *The Capital I*; and *The Condition of the Working Class in England*
- Manchester has been a centre for radical political ideas and the people were very open to it, because, as a result of involvement in the English Civil War, Manchester had no MP in Parliament
- the Church started to respond early to the social challenge by discovering the social dimension of the kingdom of God. The Labour Church Movement started in Manchester in 1891
- the industrial revolution – the Manchester Ship Canal
- birthplace of the *Guardian* newspaper.

Manchester has been a real source of inspiration and encouragement to many other UK cities, as well as to other nations. In the last few years Manchester has pioneered some exciting initiatives in Christian mission, with hundreds of churches regularly joining forces in united prayer and outreach. Soul Survivor: The Message 2000 was the first in a series of large-scale evangelistic festivals that have since happened in numerous other locations.

How would you like your community to look?

As I travel around speaking about ROC, I often ask, "How would you like your community to look in five years?"

In 1995, as our new inter-church united prayer gatherings were beginning to gain momentum, we wrote this mission statement:

> Our desire is to see the spiritual atmosphere in the region of Greater Manchester transformed. We long for a move of God

that will bring renewal and restoration to the Church and will spill over into society at large. In our dreams and visions we see crime rates dropping, violence decreasing, drug dealers disappearing, prostitution declining and apathy diminishing. We "see" business booming, housing improving, schools flourishing and hope rising. We "see" other cities across Europe looking at the evidence of the illuminating and seasoning effect of the kingdom of God.

We believe that such a reversal of the current situation will only come about as a result of God pouring out His Spirit upon a Church united in a determined commitment to seek His face. So we aim to build a fortress of effective prayer around the Greater Manchester region by helping to network together Christians from all denominations and streams.

We had no idea back then how prophetic those words would be. Let me give you a few examples.

Crime rates falling

In 2004, we held the regional launch of ROC at the Reebok Stadium in Bolton, home of the Premier League football team, Bolton Wanderers. Senior police officers, chief executives of city councils, MPs, mayors and business leaders attended, along with well over 1,000 Christians from around the region.

On that evening we heard from senior police officers about how crime was significantly falling in areas where Christians were committed to ongoing prayer. The challenge to churches everywhere is to stay in touch with the Police and to sustain concerted levels of prayer. People left the meeting feeling inspired and challenged to pray specifically.

Someone once said that "general prayer is a breeding ground for unbelief". I have come to discover the truth of those words. Do our prayers really hit the target? Are we as conscientious and deliberate about prayer as we are about preaching or mission or social action? Specific prayer, which is in the will of God and well thought through, attracts specific results. We told over 1,000 people at the Reebok, including Hazel Blears, the leaders of Sefton and Salford councils, and lots of police officers that crime would fall as a result of our prayers! I was even prompted to specify a time frame, something which is very scary. We said that within twelve months crime would fall in the North West.

The following summer an article appeared in the Friday, 24th June, 2005, edition of the *Manchester Metro News* under the banner headline "CRIME PLUMMETS BY 11 PER CENT":

> "Crime has plummeted in Greater Manchester, according to figures released by the Police. The statistics reveal a 3% reduction in violent crime – bucking the national trend. Forces bosses hailed the overall reduction of 11.5% ... as 'a tremendous achievement'."

Martin Robinson, Director of mission and theology at the Bible Society,[2] said that people often ask, "How would we recognise signs of revival in a twenty-first-century, western, post-modern culture?" One of the signs, he said, is when we hear "good news stories" reported in the media. This is certainly something we have seen increasingly in Manchester.

Housing improving

In the last ten years or so there has been a housing boom in Manchester with new developments springing up all over the city and its suburbs. The city centre has been transformed with dilapidated former mills and warehouses now reborn as designer apartments. Throughout the inner city, row upon row of worn-out housing stock has been demolished and new, sustainable and affordable properties are being offered in special schemes to local people, with teachers and hospital staff given priority.

Salford, part of Greater Manchester, is described as a city in the process of transformation as it moves into an exciting future as a thriving cultural, economic and residential location. The already successful transformation of the former derelict Salford Docks into the award-winning Salford Quays, with its diverse waterfront, has led the way in regeneration across the city. From its urbanised core to the greenbelt in the west, places are being created in Salford which people will want to visit and invest in and where people will want to live. Some of the most sought-after housing in Greater Manchester is now in Salford, where many people work and study.

At the heart of all this regeneration has been a growing network of Christians called by God to move into these areas while they were still run-down. They began to join forces to pray for community redemption way backing the 90s. Here's a brief testimony from Tania Burch, originally from the Ukraine, who has recently moved into Nadine Street in Salford:

"Several years ago, Chris Lane, the young leader of Langworthy Road Community church, and his friends started prayer walking around the area of Salford always finishing in Nadine Street. Little did they know that the Lord was getting ready to answer their prayers and touch that street in a special way.

A few years ago a Christian family moved to Nadine Street to be closer to what the Lord was doing in the World Harvest Bible Church. Very soon after that it also became a home to some missionaries from Samoa. Two doors from them there is a dormitory for male students of World Harvest Bible Training Centre, which is a part of a thriving church planted ten years ago by Pastors Matt and Julie Beemer.

We moved into the area in 2007 only to discover that the house next door but one was occupied by the Pastor of a church in Eccles and his loving family. Not far from them lives a single mother who gave her heart to the Lord.

Nadine Street is situated on the same road as Alpha Street (!), where the Lord carefully placed a family from Langworthy Community Church and also a missionary couple from America next door to them! A number of children from Nadine and Alpha Street have visited World Harvest Bible Church. Most of them invited Jesus into their heart! At the back of our house in one of the new bungalows lives a friendly Christian family who made friends with us after they saw a fish sign in our window. Neither of us discussed our denominational differences, we just rejoice at the goodness of our Lord who placed us among His own. The challenges of the inner city are still there, but what a joy it is to see the kingdom of light pushing the darkness out and redeeming our streets."

Schools flourishing

Salford has been chosen as the home for the latest government City Academy. This will be staffed and managed by the Oasis Trust and will operate initially in the redundant Hope High School. This is an answer to the prayers which Christians in Salford have prayed for many years.

Salford is the twelfth most deprived authority of the one hundred and fifty nationally. Jill Baker, Strategic Director of Children's Services for Salford City Council and a committed Christian has sent us these remarkable education statistics.

GCSE results % 5+ A*–C

Year	Salford	National
2002	36.87	50.28
2003	37.44	51.86
2004	39.28	52.92
2005	46.60	55.52
2006	52.22	58.23

Obviously you can interpret this in a number of ways, including the fact that the improvement between 2003 and 2006 has been at double the national rate.

Key Stage 2 (Tests taken by all 11 year olds at the end of primary school)
There is a strong correlation between deprivation and attainment. Therefore, the fact that we are at about the national average in English, Maths and Science is an outstanding achievement.

Attendance
School attendance has been a challenge in Salford for a number of years. However, truancy has decreased significantly recently and in 2006 Salford showed the second highest rate of improvement nationally – behind the Scilly Isles!

Jill writes, "I am encouraged by the support and interest shown to Children's Services by the churches in Salford. Local government is increasingly being encouraged to form strong partnerships with voluntary sector bodies, such as the Church. We know that in order to make a difference in our society, improving outcomes for children and young people, we have to work together.

Since I first sent these results, Salford's results have gone up to 60% 5+ A*–C for 2007! This means that we have increased from 38% to 60% in 3 years – an additional 550 young people getting 5+."

Other cities looking
We have been humbled by the number of groups of churches contacting us from all across the UK and abroad during the last ten years asking for advice on how to organise citywide prayer and outreach. I have worked with groups in Birmingham, Brighton, Blackpool, Newcastle, Sheffield, Carlisle, Chester,

Merseyside, Shropshire, Croydon, York, Southampton, London, Jersey, Sweden and, most recently, Berlin.

There is a network called "Together for Berlin". Axel Nehlsen had read our book *City-Changing Prayer* and wanted to invite me to speak at their "Transform" conference in February 2008. He and some of his team wanted to visit Manchester to see what God is doing in our city. So, in May 2007, Axel Nehlsen, Kerstin Hack, Rosemarie Streseman and Harold Sommerfeld came to visit Manchester. They attended a North West leaders' forum, a quarterly gathering of pastors and leaders from across the region, and we were able to pray for Berlin, which was an amazing highlight of the whole day for me.

Alpha Manchester [3]

In October 2007, thirty-five churches got together to run a joint Alpha course at Manchester United Football Club's International Suite. The launch party was attended by three hundred and eighty people and each Monday the course attracted over three hundred guests. At the time of writing we don't know how many have come to faith through this, but we are sure it will be a significant number. Ten years ago, such an inter-church venture would have been impossible to imagine, such was the lack of co-operation and unity. We are reminded, however, that the Lord can do immeasurably more than we can ask or imagine.

Redeeming the Arts

Since the launch of our inter-church prayer gatherings in 1993, we have repeatedly prayed for the arts and media. In 2002, we hired The Lowry theatre for a prayer gathering, which included a showcase of artists from across the region. Artists performed and displayed their work inside and outside the theatre. The Lowry kept their bars open to the public so that shoppers and passers-by could watch the performances and view the art. At the same time, over 1,500 people gathered to pray in the main theatre.

In February 2004, Redeeming the Arts (a ministry of City Links) was launched to pray specifically for artists and the media on a regular basis. Many artists feel isolated and others have found it hard to break into a very competitive market to get their work recognised and celebrated. We have seen many answers to prayer in terms of providing a support network and a place where artists can showcase their work. In the last year we have heard some amazing stories from people we have prayed for. Among them are, Becky Higg who has just recorded a CD *Room to Move*, Doug Walker, who was featured on Chris Moyles' Radio 1 breakfast show with his song *The Mystery*, and Kristina Myles who won Radio 5's *Busk Idol* and recently toured with Chris De Burgh. We have regularly prayed for Christian artists who use their music in the context of mission like Andy Smith from The Message Trust, and Mark Pennells, who is the Director of Innervation Trust,[4] with bands like Collective, bandwithnoname and TBC.

Praying for the BBC

As we continued to develop Redeeming the Arts, we sensed a growing need to pray for the BBC specifically. We discovered that the BBC was moving much of its operations to Salford, creating the first European media city. This is how the Manchester Evening News described it:

> "*NEW MEDIA CITY* – Salford Quays will be the home of Europe's first Media City! At its heart is a triangle of iconic buildings – The Lowry, Imperial War Museum North and a new media complex, future home to the BBC. The area is described as, 'A new network of tightly knit streets, squares and boulevards which will cascade down into a huge waterfront

piazza; a place to watch the sunset, enjoy a drink or a concert, and have some great conversations.' "

How exciting! And how different from the images we see on Corrie! One hugely encouraging factor is that the BBC will be formally linked to one of the new Academies which are soon to open in Salford run by Steve Chalke's Oasis Trust. I read a copy of the inscription in the entrance hall of the BBC headquarters in Portland House London, which states:

> "To Almighty God, this shrine of the arts, music and literature is dedicated by the first Governors in the year of our Lord 1931, John Reith being Director General. It is their prayer that good seed sown will produce a good harvest, that everything offensive to decency and hostile to peace will be expelled, and that the nation will incline its ear to those things which are lovely, pure and of good report and thus pursue that path of wisdom and virtue."

God enables His people to "redeem" that which belongs to Him. Our prayers for the BBC were right in line with the declaration made at its inception. Following this real push to pray for the BBC an amazing thing happened.

The Manchester Passion

In the early part of 2006, we heard that the BBC would be commissioning a major event to be broadcast live from the streets of Manchester on Good Friday, *The Manchester Passion*, a contemporary re-telling of the last few hours of Jesus' life, using popular music from the cream of Manchester bands. *The Passion* followed key moments in the Gospel story and unfolded in a procession through Manchester City Centre culminating in Albert Square. The actor who played Jesus carried a sixteen foot cross through the streets of the city.

This BBC Three event aimed to attract the non-churchgoing public and the Bishop of Manchester, the Right Reverend Nigel McCulloch, commented: "*The Manchester Passion* has a sincerity and an ability to shock and connect that is not far removed from how it must have been on the first Good Friday."

By their own confession, the performers were mostly non-churchgoing people and a real highlight for us was when Darren Morfitt, star of Dog Soldiers and the actor who played Jesus, cried out from the roof of the Town Hall in Albert Square, "I am the resurrection and the life," which for many of his hearers would invoke nothing more than the title of a song from the Manchester band The Stone Roses – but it would certainly get their attention for that reason.

Frank and I were watching the whole thing on TV along with others and we had tears rolling down our faces. Billy Kennedy, a friend from Southampton, rang to congratulate us. We were quite amused, as the whole thing had been the idea of the BBC! Prayer really had been a powerful first step though.

My friend Chip Kendall from the bandwithnoname, was at Greenbelt, a music festival held for many years over the August bank holiday, where the cast of *The Manchester Passion* told of the effect the production had had on them. This testimony has been such a confirmation of the urgency to keep praying for the BBC.

We have just heard that during Holy Week, 2008, the BBC will broadcast *The Passion,*[5] a new series which will be shown in peak time and seen by many millions of people. Jesus is played by Joseph Mawle who is seen in *Persuasion* and *Clapham Junction*. James Nesbitt plays Pilate and Darren Morfitt plays Peter. The BBC say there was no religious motive in producing the series. Quite simply they were looking for a great story to tell and the story of Jesus is an iconic story that bears retelling in every generation.

What an honour it will be to welcome them to their new home in Salford in a few years' time. And what a responsibility also to keep on praying for more redemptive breakthroughs in the lives of those who work there.

Since the launch of Redeeming the Arts in 2004, we have seen many new artists and arts ministries emerge:

Pop Connections,[6] is led by Andy Silver, who put together the 300 strong choir for the opening ceremony of the 2002 Commonwealth Games in Manchester. This is an exciting ministry linking Primary Schools with community groups by recording a pop music CD. In school time, children take part in the entire process of singing and recording a highly professional, original CD which is launched by the school with a big concert together with churches and other community groups. Out of this comes long-lasting relationships between school and community and loads of families get involved with churches. In their first year they had twenty-one projects in schools, involving 4,000 children.

MassiveUK,[7] led by Hannah Latty (née Atkins), began in 2004 and is making tremendous inroads into the arts in Manchester placing Christian musicians, bands and DJs into secular venues all across the city. Hannah recently teamed up with Steve Cole to develop "Artisan" in Manchester. Steve established Artisan over ten years ago in London with the vision of providing support to Christians involved in the music industry and has since broadened to Media, Arts and Fashion.

GENETIK – The Tribe Academy, led by Tim Owen, formerly of Worldwide Message Tribe. The vision now is to train up young people in performing arts primarily for use in evangelism. Genetik courses run twice a year for handpicked young adults and include biblical study components and a mentoring programme.[8]

It's so wonderful to be involved in praying and working for social transformation and to see before our very eyes, answers to our prayers emerging in so many different spheres of society. Redeeming our communities involves so much more than painting fences and removing graffiti. God is calling

His people to clean up and renew every aspect of the world in which we live: education, healthcare, politics, business, media, fashion, sport – wherever we find ourselves, there's work to be done in advancing His kingdom, and, as we pray and step out in faith, we'll find there are like-minded co-believers quite close by as well. I've lost count of the number of times people have shared with me that they had discovered they had been sharing an office with a Christian brother or sister for years and didn't realise it until some sort of mission initiative stirred them into action. I thank God for all He's done in Manchester thus far, but I need to keep reminding myself that there is plenty more still to do to see the kind of glorious transformation He plans for our communities.

Recently Premier Radio rang to ask me about the latest shooting in Moss Side. Every time that happens I know that evil still has an expression and we are motivated to pray all the more. In June 2008 we will host another mega prayer meeting to pray for our communities and trust that more prayer will mean less violence and hope will arise.

In August 2007, as I sat watching News 24 and another death on Moss Side was reported, there was a small glimmer of hope. The Police and the Street Pastors walked out side by side to say that they are working together so that these things become a part of our history, not our future. I started to sense a renewed challenge to pray specifically into this. Manchester is a work in progress.

Notes

1. *The Condition of the Working-Class in England in 1844* (London: Swan Sonnenschein & Co., 1892), p. 45.
2. www.biblesociety.org.uk
3. www.alphamanchester.org
4. www.innervation.org
5. www.churchesmediacouncil.org.uk/passion
6. www.popconnection.co.uk
7. www.massiveuk.org.uk
8. See www.message.org.uk/genetik

Redeeming Our Communities – the National Launch

Following the regional launch of Redeeming Our Communities in the North West in 2004, we were being encouraged by Christian leaders to roll out the initiative across the country. It was a daunting prospect! How would we go about communicating the message of ROC around the nation?

The message of ROC is about transforming communities through prayer, action and partnership. Prayer as the foundation, action as the practical outpouring and partnership as the most effective vehicle to achieve community transformation. We knew that the national launch had to be based on the same principles as the initiative itself, so we set about building on and developing partnerships with the Police, churches and Christian organisations who all shared the common aim of seeing crime and disorder reduced and communities transformed.

In the run up to the launch we formalised partnerships with over twenty-five Christian organisations local churches and of course, the Police.[1] One of the main partnerships we formed was with the World Prayer Centre,[2] based in Birmingham and headed up by Ian and Pauline Cole. My good friend Jane Holloway was also based with WPC as the Prayer Co-ordinator. Jane and I share a long history of promoting the importance of prayer in transforming our communities.

Through Jane, I discovered that WPC were running prayer events at the National Exhibition Centre in Birmingham called Trumpet Call. These events were a call to Christians across the UK to pray for the nations of the world.

Divine appointments

In 2005 I went to Stoke-on-Trent to speak at a Youth For Christ[3] event and afterwards met with Lloyd Cooke from Saltbox.[4] Lloyd, who is on the organising team of the Trumpet Call events, also planted the idea that I should visit Ian Cole to share the vision of ROC. Talks began with Ian and Jane about using the Trumpet Call events to launch the ROC initiative nationally. Our friends at the World Prayer Centre were amazingly supportive of the vision and agreed to host the national launch on the 13th May, 2006, as part of their Trumpet Call programme at the NEC. What an answer to prayer! Without them, the launch just would not have been possible and I am indebted to their investment in the initiative. Around the same time as these talks were taking place I was invited by Paul Ellis, a police chaplain from Sheffield, to visit his friend, Matt Baggott, the Chief Constable of Leicestershire Police. Paul had been meeting with Matt for several years and he invited me to accompany him. Matt was enthusiastic about the vision of ROC and agreed to be at the launch event.

We now had our deadline in place and the countdown began. Following the same format of the regional launch at the Reebok stadium in Bolton, I was keen to replicate a number of key areas: a fast moving programme to inspire and encourage all those who attended the event, the invitation of Police representatives, local councillors and politicians, and to provide quality resources to help people put into practice the things they had heard as they returned to their own communities. The task list was really overwhelming and it felt like God was asking the impossible of us.

The power of saying "thank you"

One of the first ideas that had helped lay the foundation for the ROC initiative was to say "thank you" to Police officers for all the work they do on our behalf, by putting up posters in local Police stations around Greater Manchester back in 1998. We have always prioritised inviting secular agencies to our meetings so that we can say thank you, pray for them and demonstrate that we, as Christians, support the work they do. We had successfully invited VIPs to the regional launch and I was keen to continue this for the national launch by inviting Police, local council and politicians so that we could share knowledge and experience, and celebrate together all the good work being done to transform communities by secular agencies and Christians alike. Over 500 invitations went out across the nation and we began the nervous wait for responses. They began to trickle back in, and then, to our surprise, the trickle became a flood! We received over 150 positive responses from police officers, politicians and local council officers including Mike Whitby, Leader of Birmingham City Council, Caroline Spelman MP and Matt Baggott, Chief Constable of Leicestershire Police.

One of our invitations was sent to David Cameron, leader of the Conservative Party. Unfortunately he was not able to attend the event due to family commitments, but he sent us the following endorsement of our work and the launch event:

"I am delighted to lend my support to the Redeeming Our Communities initiative. We all have a shared responsibility for our shared future. Individuals, families, government, business, and voluntary organisations all have a vital role to play. Redeeming Our Communities shows how such values can be put into practice. In areas where it has been working in partnership with the Police and other agencies, the Police have recognised how beneficial that work can be. The national launch is an exciting opportunity to extend such partnerships elsewhere, so that other communities too can be helped. Many have cause to be grateful for all you have done. May I pay tribute to everyone involved in this work up to now and wish you well for the Birmingham launch event in May. I am sure it will be a great success."

I was delighted with the responses from the VIPs and the support they were showing for the initiative, but the work did not finish there. We were keen to develop and formalise our partnerships with the various organisations, including the Neighbourhood Policing Project[5] which you will hear more about in Chapter 7. We invited each of our partners to join us at The Message Trust[6] offices in Manchester for a Partners' Day in April and were thrilled when over fifty representatives from the partner organisations arrived in sunny (well, it wasn't raining!) Manchester for a day of thanksgiving, prayer and discussion as to how we could all work together and support one another in the things we were doing. We celebrated the things that were going on across the country as we heard from each organisation and then spoke about how we would take this forward and where ROC fitted into the picture. This whole day was a taster of what we were expecting at the National Launch and I was getting excited.

Tools for the task

Another of our key areas of focus was the commitment to resourcing all those who wanted to do more in their communities and so we set upon the idea of producing a Resource Tool DVD to be given out, free of charge, to each delegate who attended the conference to take back to their communities to use in small groups and local churches. This tool would include footage from the regional launch, interviews with key Christian leaders, information from all our partners and pointers to help everyone to pray effectively for their communities. I knew that this tool was significant and as such, it presented us with the most problems. One of my Trustees, Robert Varnam, invested many hours into the production of the DVD, but continually had problems with computers crashing and formatting issues. We called on the intercessors to pray and eventually, through much prayer and hard work, the DVD was ready. However, our anxious wait continued as there was a three week turn-around for the final production which meant that it should be ready on the Thursday, 11th May, just two days before the launch. We could not afford anything to go wrong so we kept praying.

Alongside the Resource Tool DVD, a key element of the day was going to be a top quality exhibition, featuring organisations that were working in communities, to offer advice and practical resources as to how to actually go about transforming your community. Again this was not my area of expertise, but I was able to call on a fantastic lady called Debbie Doran who had organised the exhibition at Merseyfest in Liverpool in 2005. Debbie is one of those people who just gets on and does things and never seems to panic. She was such a blessing to us and undertook the whole organisation of the exhibition in the run up to the event and on the day itself, even getting up at 5 a.m. on the day of the event to get to the NEC in time to greet the exhibitors.

A vicar's dream

It was a few days before the national launch when I received a call from Nick Bundock, Vicar of St James and Emmanuel Church in Didsbury. We were experiencing a really busy and stressful week as we had lots of last minute things to do before the event. At times like that, we needed God to remind us about why we were doing all the work. The phone rang and my friend Nick said, "I've had a dream which I believe is for you." In his dream, he had seen a huge traffic jam. Cars were hemmed in on every side and nothing was moving. Drivers looked frustrated and helpless. (At this point I will resist telling any jokes about the M25!) Nick "saw" a lone police officer seeking to direct the traffic, but with little success. Then the officer lifted his right arm towards the centre of the jam and began to pray, "Come, Lord Jesus." He repeated the phrase over and over. The scene panned out to reveal hundreds of people all with arms raised towards the police officer calling out in prayer, "Come, Lord Jesus." As they did, the traffic began to move and the roads were clear. Nick woke up at that point and noticed his own arm was raised. He felt as though electricity was running up and down his arm. He was convinced that the dream was significant and that it related to ROC and our calling to pray for the Police. He said that although he could not be at the NEC he felt he should tell me about his dream. I thanked him, but wondered whether he had been eating too much cheese the night before! Catching myself, I repented and promised God I would be on the lookout for some sort of connection on the day.

The big day dawns

Finally, that big day arrived and what an amazing occasion it was. It started as these days often do, with things going wrong. I arrived at the NEC with two of my most valued team members, Wendy Ashcroft and Catherine Proudman, only to be refused access to the Arena as our names were not down on the security guard's list. We did finally make it into the arena and then heard that there had been several accidents on the motorway which were holding up people trying to get to the NEC. The crowds did start to trickle in and eventually around seven thousand turned up to join in the launch of ROC nationally as part of the Trumpet Call prayer event.

It was wonderful to welcome around one hundred and fifty VIPs for a special lunch reception followed by the presentation itself. After lunch we were ushered into the main arena for the launch programme, a one and a half hour presentation. The programme was split into three parts: the causes of crime, stories about "Cops and Robbers" and prayer and policing in partnership. We were challenged and encouraged by speakers including Malcolm Duncan,[7] leader of Faithworks,[8] and Caroline Spelman MP, Chair of the Conservative Party, to hear stories of what Christians can be involved in and the vital role that we can and should be playing in our communities. There were some funny moments, like the apparently miraculous appearance of a blue foam pop shield on the microphone handed to Caroline (a Conservative) as she stepped up to the platform (until this point, every other microphone had sported a bright red pop shield). She looked pleasantly surprised, smiled wryly, thanked whoever had made the timely switch and then shared powerfully about the need for Christians to be at work in the community.

Youth: problem and solution

In the "causes of crime" section we learned two interesting facts about young people in the UK. Firstly, that they are responsible for more crime than any other sector of the population,[9] and secondly, the largest single provider of youth work in the UK is the Christian Church. Matt Wilson and Andy Hawthorne from The Message Trust recounted some stirring stories of how their long-term outreach projects in the toughest areas of Manchester are not only changing the lives of young people, but also seeing these youngsters becoming part of the solution as they take responsibility for transforming their own communities. We celebrated the fact that the Church is the biggest provider of youth services in the UK, but were spurred on to do more.

Cops and Robbers

We then moved on to our "Cops and Robbers" section and heard from those who were working directly with men and women in prisons and with offenders once they had been released. We heard that a recent British Home Office document has suggested that 7% of offenders account for 65% of offences. This particular group consists of both the most dangerous criminals, who repeatedly commit violent offences, and the most expensive criminals in terms of the cost to society of repeated prison terms.[10] These can be some of the most hardened and chaotic people to work with.[11] I was joined on stage by organisations such as Re:Flex[12] and Offenders Anonymous[13] who are committed to supporting these key individuals. Roy Crowne, National Director of Youth For Christ, spoke about prisoners whose lives were being transformed by their "Mettle" discipleship courses, of which there are currently 700. We also heard from PC Bob Collier (his story is in Chapter 5), and reformed robber Damian, of how God had turned their lives around.

Damian said,

> "These Christian guys just got alongside me and showed me how to live a life of faith. They helped me to live a life free from drink and drug addiction. Just to cut a long story short, my life was radically transformed. I'm now happily married for two years, I've got a beautiful baby boy, and I have had the privilege of leading three members of my own family to Jesus."

These were amazing and moving testimonies of God's transforming power. I don't think anyone who heard those testimonies could have failed to be affected. (Incidentally, you can see and hear these testimonies on the ROC DVD which is available from the website.)

The last section of our programme was devoted to partnering with the Police. I was joined by Matt Baggott, Chief Constable of Leicestershire Police, who has been a supporter and advocate of ROC over many years now. Matt is part of the national leadership of the Neighbourhood Policing Programme, which is currently being rolled out across the country. As a Christian, Matt freely acknowledges that the Holy Spirit initiates and works through initiatives such as Neighbourhood Policing. What a blessing to have him in such a position of responsibility and influence. He is being used mightily by God in his work. The idea of Neighbourhood Policing is to create permanent and dedicated teams in every local neighbourhood that will focus on problems that the community has told the Police matter most to them. In this section of the programme we were also joined by Don Axcell, Executive Director of the Christian Police Association,[14] who was encouraging us to commit to praying for the Police and for specific needs in our communities through initiatives such as Adopt-A-Cop. Don told us that three churches in Hampshire had been praying for the Police and had seen a 30% reduction in crime. Praying and policing in partnership is what ROC is all about.

Come, Lord Jesus

As a final act of prayer, we wanted to pray for the police officers who were present. Ian Cole had warned me it might be a big challenge practically to ask them to come forward in such a packed arena, but it seemed important. Officers and civilians walked out to the front. It was a moving moment especially as we remembered officers who had lost their lives in the line of duty, including our own friend from Manchester, Stephen Oake. We began to pray for those assembled at the front and an amazing thing happened. I looked up and saw hundreds of arms outstretched towards the police officers at the front and people calling out, "Come, Lord Jesus." Nick's dream was happening right at that moment and I knew the impact would be dramatic. A few weeks later we heard that a senior police officer who had no church background had given his life to the Lord. He said later, "No one had ever said thank you to me in that way or shown me appreciation in the way I experienced on that day."

One of the ROC Steering Group members and Trustee of The Message Trust, Colin Hardicre, wrote the following about the event:

> "The launch was unforgettable with the worship, the testimonies, the prayers and especially the prayers for the Police when dozens of serving officers stood in front of the stage while 7,000 of us prayed over them. The Lord was there. Although I know of some lives that were transformed that day, none of us will ever know the eternal consequences of that touch from the King, at least not this side of Heaven. Through my involvement with the World Prayer Centre, The Message and ROC, I have seen God's army on the move and it is gathering pace. I know that ROC is a key part of this movement as praying and policing in partnership starts to help reclaim our towns and cities."

Ian Cole adds his comments:

> "When we started the Trumpet Call prayer journey for the nation in 2003, the first area God led us into was to pray for a lifting of the oppression from the land and an awakening of the sleeping giant, the Church, in the land. Little did we know that three Trumpet Calls later we would be partnering with Debra and her team from Manchester in the National launch of ROC.
>
> We can now look back and see that God, in answer to our prayers and the prayers of Christians over many years, is encouraging, prodding and sometimes pushing His Church

into that awakening to go and be Good News across the nations.

ROC is a growing, going movement giving a lead across communities to see significant reduction in crime, a restoration of hope and dignity, and through prayer and action creating the spiritual climate that heralds God's kingdom coming and His will being done on the streets as it is in Heaven."

I don't think I'll ever fully know the impact of that day on people's lives and in people's communities, but I know that it acted as a catalyst for many, including us, to pursue the ROC agenda.

Steering straight ahead

We set about developing the concept of ROC so that it could be used by any city, town and village across the country. We gathered a group of key leaders to form the steering group that would act as a strategic advisory and visionary group to set the course for the initiative. I remember the first time we met together, representatives from the Police, churches and Christian organisations, all drawn together by a common desire to see communities transformed. It was such an amazing time as we refined the vision of ROC and heard from some very wise people.[15] I must admit to being a little bit daunted going into the meeting, but I was completely inspired on leaving the meeting by everything people had to say.

One of our main discussion points through the meeting was to ensure the distinctiveness and professionalism of ROC. All those in the meeting believed that the main priority should be to focus on the key aspect of prayer and policing in partnership. This is the aspect that sets ROC apart and it became our main focus for development in the following months. We were determined to build a strong, positive, two-way partnership with the Police, which we believed needed to be founded on trust.

I was struck by words from Matt Baggott and Kevin Borg, both serving Police officers and also on our steering group, that we needed to *invest in building a partnership based on trust with the Police*. We needed to reassure them that Police officers are not our Christian targets, but that we genuinely want to work with them. We need to ensure that our words translate into action and that what we say we'll do, we actually do. We also need to ensure that we are professional in everything we do and not bombard them with over-enthusiastic Christians.

Nuts and Bolts

As part of the national launch programme I had committed ROC to producing resources and guidelines to be used by anyone in their city, town and village across the country. The only problem was that at that time, we didn't have any! I asked my PA at the time, Catherine Proudman, to develop some guidelines in line with best practice to help build this partnership of trust with the Police based on our own experiences, and the vision of ROC for the future. What resulted are the Step by Step guidelines that you can download from the City Links website today.[16] This resource gives practical information on how you can begin to get involved in your communities. Our vision for ROC is that it will mirror the Neighbourhood Policing structure across the country so that in every Police force and area within the force there are ROC representatives working in partnership with the Police.

Following these guidelines we have also produced another two Resource DVDs, one that features footage of the national launch and one that is based on prayer and how to pray for our communities. In addition we have been encouraged to run a conference for ROC called "Nuts and Bolts".[17] This is for people who say, "Yes, I want to be involved in my community, but how do I actually go about that?" Our first conference took place at Regents Theological College, Nantwich, in June 2007 and our second will be held at Ashburnham Place, East Sussex, in April 2008. These times are great opportunities to spend time with others who share similar visions and the same commitment to see their communities transformed.

Notes

1. Partners of Redeeming Our Communities: World Prayer Centre (www.worldprayer.org.uk), The Message Trust (www.message.org.uk), Prayer Week (www.i61.org/prayerweek), Faithworks (www.faithworks.info), 24-7 Prayer (www.24-7prayer.com), Evangelical Alliance (www.eauk.org), Street Pastors (www.streetpastors.org.uk), UCB (www.ucb.co.uk), Community Watchmen Ministries/Drugsnet (drugsnet@hotmail.com), Christian Aid (www.christianaid.org.uk), The Saltbox Community Church (www.saltbox.org.uk), The Shaftesbury Society (www.shaftesburysoc.org.uk), Christians Against Poverty (www.capuk.org), Prayer.tv (www.prayerinaction.net), CPA (www.cpauk.net), Speak (www.speak.org.uk), The Light Project (www.lightproject.org.uk), Gateway Christian Media (www.gatewaymedia.org.uk), Together for the Harvest (www.tfh.org.uk), The Nationwide Christian Trust (www.nationwidechristiantrust.com), Alpha (uk.alpha.org), Church Action on Poverty (www.church-poverty.org.uk), Bible Society (www.biblesociety.org.uk), Church Urban Fund (www.cuf.org.uk), Ambassadors in Sport (www.aisint.org).
2. www.worldprayer.org.uk
3. www.yfc.co.uk
4. www.saltbox.org.uk
5. www.neighbourhoodpolicing.co.uk
6. www.message.org.uk
7. Malcolm has written a book on local church and community: Malcolm Duncan, *Kingdom Come* (Lion Hudson, ISBN: 978-1-854247-98-8).
8. www.faithworks.info
9. According to Home Office statistics, the peak age for offending for males in England and Wales was 18 in 1997–98. 9% of 18 year old males were found guilty of, or cautioned for, an indictable offence in that year. For females, rates of offending were lower and the peak age was younger at 15: 2% of 15 year old females offended in 1997–98. These peak ages have changed over time. Before 1972 the peak age of offending for both males and females was 14; this rose to 15 for males following the raising of the

school leaving age from 15 to 16 in 1972. By 1988 the peak age for males had risen to 18 while that for females fluctuated between 14 and 15. In 1997–98, the peak age for male offending in Northern Ireland was 19, and 14% of this group were found guilty of an offence at the Crown Court or magistrate's court. The equivalent peak for females was age 18, and 2% of this group were found guilty of an offence (www.homeoffice.gov.uk).

10. www.offenders-anonymous.org.uk
11. www.homeoffice.gov.uk/rds/pdfs07/hosb1107.pdf
12. www.reflexuk.net
13. www.offenders-anonymous.org.uk
14. www.cpauk.net
15. The ROC Steering Group is currently: Kevin Borg (West Midlands Police and founder of the New Hope Mentoring Programme), David Muir (Public Policy Director for Evangelical Alliance), Malcolm Duncan (leader of Faithworks), Colin Hardicre (Trustee of The Message Trust), Nick Cuthbert (Riverside Church, Birmingham), Frank Green (Operations Director for The Message Trust), Jane Holloway (World Prayer Centre) and Matt Baggott (Chief Constable of Leicestershire Police).
16. See Appendix 1 of Chapter 7, "Praying and Policing in Partnership".
17. Details at www.citylinks.org.uk

Prayer and Social Transformation

Prayer is popular

It may surprise you to learn that prayer is popular, even among non-churchgoing people. A poll of 2,000 British adults, commissioned by the charity Tearfund for Global Poverty Week in November 2007,[1] revealed that prayer is considered a vital part of life by nearly half of UK adults, with 20 million people (about 42% of the population) saying they pray regularly, and one in three believing that, "God is watching over them".

Pete Greig, founder of 24-7 Prayer,[2] comments:

> "One of the surprising discoveries we've made since 24-7 began is this: people who don't want to be preached at still want to be prayed for ... Millions of non-churchgoers in the UK really do believe in the power of prayer to change the world and they pray on a regular basis: **1 in 5 adults believe that 'prayer changes the world'**. 9 million adults will pray today as they do every day ... A whopping 12 million adults believe that prayer can change the lives of their friends and family ... These statistics confirm something we already suspected ... I could show you the walls of our little prayer room in Ibiza, papered with 2,500 prayer requests gathered

from the supposed hedonists partying on the streets outside
... The fact that so many non-churchgoers believe in the
power of prayer presents us with an exciting opportunity for
inclusion."[3]

Over the last fifteen years there has been an incredible rise in
the number of Christians who are devoting time to prayer,
not only around the world, but also in the UK. It's like a tidal
wave of prayer has begun building on the foundations of
prayer that have been laid in our nation, not only down the
centuries, but more recently since the 1960s and 1970s as new
prayer organisations were started and God's Spirit was poured
out in new ways. People are meeting to pray in their homes,
in their communities, in their workplaces and in their
churches. People from different churches are meeting with
those from other churches in villages, towns, boroughs
and cities. Representatives from cities are meeting with other
cities to pray. People are meeting to pray across counties,
across regions and cities are connecting with each other in
prayer. There is a prayer network on the Isle of Man and
on Jersey, prayer mobilization taking place across Ireland,
Scotland and Wales and in every county in England.

Does prayer make a difference?

Is there evidence to back up that prayer works? As we look
back into our history, the Great Awakening or revival in the
eighteenth century occurred at a time when the Moravian
community began praying 24/7 for one hundred years,
sending out missionaries to many nations of the world. At
the same time, Jonathan Edwards called for seven years of
prayer worldwide for a spiritual awakening and his prayers
were answered! The revival in the eighteenth century came at
a time when alcoholism, social decay and moral corruption
dominated Britain.

As we move through the twenty-first century with rising levels of marital breakdown, drug abuse, crime and alcoholism that closely parallels that of the eighteenth century, God is again calling His people to the place of prayer for "History is silent about revivals that did not begin in prayer."[4]

God is stirring the desire to pray once again. It's for the people we know: our families, friends, neighbours and work colleagues. Prayer is being mobilized for leaders in communities: church leaders, community leaders and elected government officials both local and nation. Prayer is being mobilized in most of the spheres of society, including politics, education, the family, marriages, arts, media and entertainment industries, health service and the business community.

This praying spans most of the traditions of the Christian Church, It can be silent and reflective, based around prayer stations. It can be more vocal, based around worship. Over the last few years many creative prayer initiatives have been started, including prayer walls, houses of prayer, weeks of prayer, prayer walking, prayer tents and healing rooms where Christian prayer is offered for any who wish to come and ask. And God is answering this prayer in remarkable ways.

Prayer is effective

The following examples are intended to show a flavour of what God has done and is doing as He calls His people back to the place of prayer. For it is in the place of seeking His face in worship and prayer that hearts are changed by the Holy Spirit prompting action to meet current issues and needs. Prayer gives birth to faith, to unity and most importantly to vision, and it is out of vision that social action projects are begun, and out of these that social transformation can begin, redeeming our communities for God.

24-7 Prayer

This movement began in September 1999 after a church in Chichester decided to pray non stop for a month. Eight years later, it is now an international movement spawning social action and community all over the world. "A missionary movement founded on prayer", 24-7 Prayer has reached and affected Ibiza, Boys Town, Kansas, Vancouver, and many other places around the globe. The 24-7 website[5] tells "life stories" of healing, restoration and lives being committed to God during the 24-7 prayer initiative. It has swept the globe with incredible pace and is an incredible example of God's people responding faithfully to His calling to go. Prayer rooms have been set up and are spilling out in a diverse range of places, including city centres, New Age fairs and skate parks.

Ryton, in Tyne and Wear were overjoyed with the five hundred and seventy visits to their prayer room from the eight and a half thousand population. The impact of the prayer initiative in this town has been amazing. Tom Jamieson, from the prayer room in Ryton comments:

> "We're shattered, elated, grateful, and waking up to the urgency of responding to this thirst for God which we hardly believed was there in this rather sleepy, small town. We four churches do a twice yearly mail drop to every house in town so our 24-7 got a mention in the May edition and the end-of-August edition majored on it.
>
> We have good links with our local schools and this resulted in me being invited into the Comprehensive to take all the year-group assemblies the week before, to let students know what we were up to and give them a gentle invitation to drop by if they wished.
>
> The three Primary schools of the town all opted to do an afternoon workshop on Christian Prayer for their Year Six classes at our venue, where one of the round of activities would of course be spending some time in smaller groups in

the Prayer Room. But in the end it was children and young people who were making the invitations ... Some of the year six children came back after school with their parents and siblings; some of the Christian students at the comp brought their friends during lunch breaks and then those friends brought other friends.

By Friday the Headteacher's PA was with us because, as she said, 'Students are telling staff that they mustn't miss the Prayer Room so I thought I'd better come.'

Jimmy, a believer all his life, had never opened his mouth in a prayer meeting. Even as a steward at his church he had always got someone else to, 'Say the vestry prayer with the minister' as it was just too daunting for him. Well you've guessed it, Jimmy, aged 84, prayed out loud for the first time in his life in our Prayer Room. He said afterwards, 'It just seemed such a natural thing to do there.' He said next day to a friend of his, 'Bill, I'm a new man!'

The last night of our prayer week, unlike the previous nights, was quiet, with just me and Ben, aged 19, staying over. One thing we did was pray through all the written prayers left in the 'Sheep Fold' (that's what we had instead of a wailing wall). We took it in turns to read and pray them out loud. Fifty minutes of this and we were emotionally exhausted and realised we were only two thirds through. So Ben laid hands on the lot of them and did the business.

A lighter note: We had a 'sky' where you posted clouds of thanksgiving prayer. No blue left! Among them was this: 'Thank you, God, for hot men – I know it's frivolous, but it's great having them around!'"

Prayer week [6]

Prayer week began in May 2002 with just two people "prayer-walking" their town in North Wales. God is moving His people to pray like never before. Prayer Week has grown from the grass roots upwards, starting eight years ago in

North Wales with just two churches and now encompassing simply thousands of churches all over the UK and now in over seventy nations of the world. Its focus is encouraging unity: *Christian standing with Christian, Church standing with Church, Nation standing with Nation* and mobilizing prayer for people to come to know Jesus Christ. The founders of Prayer Week have now started a church in a pub and are reaching out to many with the Good News of Jesus.

Northern Ireland

In Northern Ireland there has been a foundation of prayer that serves as the bedrock of what is happening in the Church today. Ministries such as the Christian Renewal Centre, Restoration Ministries and Divine Healing Ministries have been praying and working towards Church unity and reconciliation for over thirty years. As a result of this we can see God moving and building a greater unity amongst the Body of Christ in Northern Ireland, enabling kingdom vision for towns, city and community transformation.

Inspired by George Otis Jr's *Transformations* videos, Transformations Ireland[7] has been working towards encouraging unity and community transformation since the late 1990s. This has included prayer breakfasts at which there have been opportunities to pray with those in influential roles in the province including the Chief Constable for Northern Ireland, the speaker of the Northern Ireland Assembly and Northern Ireland's Youth and Children's Commissioner. Out of these prayer breakfasts came the invitation to gather people from across the denominations to pray for the politicians at Stormont. These prayer meetings happen on a bi-monthly basis and have been challenging and inspiring, envisioning people with the need to pray *"for . . . all those in authority"* (see 1 Timothy 2:1–2).

As an outcome of the connection at Stormont, there was opportunity to host two consecutive years of the Global Day of Prayer in the grounds of the government buildings. These provided an opportunity to gather many people from different expressions of the Church across Northern Ireland with the desire to see God move in the churches and communities that were represented, and to pray for breakthrough in the difficult political situation. During these gatherings there was a particular focus on praying for social transformation with information provided by the local Police and Social Services. Direct answers to prayer surrounding these issues were seen in the quietest marching season for over thirty years in July 2006 and the largest cannabis drug haul ever in Northern Ireland. On the political front there has been dramatic change and many feel this is God at work in response to the prayers of the Church.

In Northern Ireland, prayer and social action is happening on a scale like never before as churches come together with a desire to be outward looking and bless the community where they are based. One of the major influences in this widespread movement has been Streetreach,[8] a part of the yearly youth festival "Summer Madness". Thousands of young people have been inspired by this social action mission and have carried it back to their home towns and communities, e.g. Xpression Portadown,[9] Spark Ballymena,[10] gLo Lurgan[11] and MorEdge Ballynahinch. All of these initiatives have sought to be centred on prayer, believing that prayer and social action can mean transformation. (Summer Madness is mentioned again in Chapter 6, "The Festival Model: International".)

Throughout the province there have been many prayer watches and these have taken many different formats. For seven years "Engage" in Coleraine has been facilitating worship and prayer bringing people together from different expressions of Church. As they have been faithful in pursuing what God has asked them to do, they have seen people come in from the streets and meet Jesus, and they have also witnessed God's healing power on the streets. Emotional and spiritual healing have also been evident as the Church comes together to pray and worship. This has been apparent through a marked reduction in the suicide rate in Coleraine.

Many are thankful for the foundation and inheritance of prayer that Northern Ireland has and as a new generation rises, it is anticipated that they will continue with a passion to pray and seek God for a complete transformation in this province and beyond.

Stoke-on-Trent

In 2001, a secular study looking at various socio-economic indicators in all 376 towns and cities in England and Wales placed Stoke-on-Trent at the bottom of the list. The unenviable title of "the worst place to live in the country" proved to be a catalyst for a number of Christian leaders to meet together in order to pray for the area.

In a spirit of humility and quiet desperation, the leaders asked God for His divine intervention. A subsequent city prayer gathering was arranged based on 2 Chronicles 7:14. This proved to be a powerful evening as 200 Christians gathered to cry out for God's mercy. Such was the impact of the event that similar united prayer gatherings started to take place each month under the banner of "2C7". These evening meetings were then supplemented by monthly half days of prayer and fellowship for leaders and specific weeks and months of 24/7 prayer involving numerous churches in North Staffordshire.

Some six years later, the 2C7 meetings are still going strong and have provided a platform for greater unity across the Body of Christ. This networking has become the foundation from which large, citywide evangelistic healing missions have been co-ordinated and a number of mercy ministries developed. Much of the prayer has been focused outside the Church and aimed at different societal issues. A theme of both the monthly leaders' meetings and the evening prayer gatherings has been to welcome and listen to various strategic secular leaders. As Christians have started to "humble themselves, pray and seek God's face" for local education, political, crime and health needs, so we have begun to note a series of "good news stories" emerge in these areas.

In 2006, a Faith Action Audit highlighting the community work of faith groups across the city also added to the growing sense of appreciation that many secular leaders have for the work of the Church. Christian leaders are aware of growing favour and the interest of those outside of the Church. The development of Christian radio and media organisations in the city has also been the cause of much gratitude and encouragement.

There is a growing sense that community transformation will only come about after there has been a foundation of real community engagement and connectivity. Many Christians believe that the increasing numbers of green shoots are pointing to a "new day" that is beginning to dawn across Stoke-on-Trent.

Swansea – City Prayer

This project began as clear call from God as a result of a Norwegian church leader talking of a citywide project that had been undertaken in Bergen in 2003. It had been based on the original initiative of Ed Silvoso. The goals of the project were to:

- Pray for every person in the city by name – each Christian praying personally for their circle of friends
- Pray for every city leader by name through regular prayer breakfasts where city leaders were invited to speak about the needs of the city.

Lighthouse Groups of praying people are now meeting across the city praying for their communities and seeking to meet the needs of their community. Through prayer breakfasts excellent contacts have been made with the Police, Health Service, Education and even with Swansea football and rugby clubs! During 2008, Street Pastors will commence in the centre of the city with the support of the Police and the City Council!

After praying about crime, they saw an immediate 9% reduction in crime in the city. One street which had been notorious for car theft has not had any reported car crime since. Following prayer for economic regeneration, the prosperity of the city has had a clear upturn with some major companies coming to the city, including Amazon.

Jersey

The Jersey Prayer Network began in 2000 with the aim to foster unity among leaders and people by raising "lighthouses" of united, praying Christians in the twelve parishes of Jersey, which was achieved within twelve months. The second aim was to hold united, all-island prayer gatherings concentrating on issues of concern. Currently, three prayer focus nights happen three times a year. At present, ten out of twelve parishes have an active monthly "Lighthouse" meeting.

Out of these prayer meetings, a passion for transformation of the island's society was born. In 2002 Jersey Prayer Canopy was established with the aim of recruiting Christians willing to pray for their neighbourhood, parish, and the island for the same hour of the one hundred and sixty eight hour week, every week. They currently have fifty percent of their target hours covered. Prayer ideas are prepared and distributed monthly. Christians in Jersey have enjoyed many answers to prayer and mission has been borne out of the prayer. As a direct answer to prayer, a small estate plagued with youth vandalism has been transformed. A group "prayer-walked" the entire area and not long afterwards, a man, not known to be a Christian, who lived there, recruited children to clean up the area, plant flower beds and set up football teams and competitions. A minister has declared that this should be the model for other estates. They also believe that local Police made a large drugs haul in direct response to prayer.

In the summer of 2007 Frank and I had a few days holiday in sunny Jersey. A break away from the city, the computer, the phone and the kids – a nice quiet few days to ourselves, or so we thought. On our second day my mobile rang. It was a friend, Peter Cushen, who lives near St Helier, asking if I would like him to try and arrange an appointment to see the Chief Constable. I said, "Yes," secretly thinking there would be no chance. Two hours later we found ourselves in the office of Graham Power, the island's Chief Officer! We told him about ROC and the impact it was having in terms of crime reduction and he was genuinely interested. One thing he stressed was the need for churches to co-operate if they were going to work with the Police. He had been approached over the years by a number of different churches and had decided long ago that he would not take seriously any approaches from churches that were not working together with a properly thought-through strategy – the very thing that ROC is helping to enable!

We fed back these comments to some friends of ours, Mike and Pat Field, who for years have been central to the work of the Jersey Evangelical Alliance and Nick France, leader of Christians Together in Jersey.[12] A meeting was planned for Frank and me to return to Jersey in December to address a gathering of Christians from across all the twelve parishes. We had an excellent evening together sharing vision and praying towards the next steps. God is clearly moving things forward in Jersey.

York

The city walls will be crowned in glory and from the gates there were red carpets streaming out into the communities around them with the message that the people were to go out into the community and bring the people into the kingdom of God.

Andy Hawthorne and I were invited to speak at a leaders' gathering organised by One Voice York[13] in October 2006. I received the vision described above and to my surprise the churches responded over the following Easter period by laying lengths of red carpet out in the city centre for people to walk across. Cards were given out and this presented a unique opportunity to talk to them about God's love and why each one of them was so special. The Archbishop of York, together with several pastors, performed twenty one open-air, full immersion baptisms. A Jewish lady came to faith and was immediately baptized by the Archbishop of York.

This was an unprecedented public demonstration of Christian unity which could not have been possible had it not been for years of prayers across denominational boundaries, the development of relationships, and much of the ground work laid by One Voice York. This initiative gave birth to a prayer movement beginning with three leaders committing to pray together for the city. Today they are joined by thirty to fifty leaders meeting together every week for one hour. There are also occasional prayer breakfasts with city dignitaries and they have recently prayed with the Chief Inspector for neighbourhood policing and the Police Superintendent for central area of North Yorkshire. There is goodwill from local authorities and Police, with a genuine desire to work together for the good of communities. For the last three years the York Minster has hosted the Global Day of Prayer[14] events at Pentecost which has helped to foster unity and partnership across the region.

One Voice York say that that they have seen greater potential for projects released when churches work together under the same banner. They have a number of social action projects: "Refresh" – a youth café, "FUSE" – a bimonthly nightclub and provider of evangelism training for children over fourteen, a student website, a school of theology which uses many church premises, the York Christian Heritage Walk

– hosted by volunteers combining a guide around historical sights with an opportunity to share the Gospel.

Wandsworth

Wandsworth, in South West London has a diverse population where those who are affluent live almost side-by-side with those who are socially deprived. Prayernet began in response to this social divide, initially with just four women representing different denominations praying in unity, and has grown significantly over the eight years since its conception. Prayer meetings gave birth to vision and this vision culminated in 2005 with the borough hosting an "On the Move" Mission, bringing worship and barbecues to central Wandsworth. In 2007 this event had grown and eighteen hundred burgers were given out, some even cooked by the Mayor. Many people totally unconnected with the Church still talk about these events.

On the seventh day of the seventh month in 2007, Christians gathered in the town hall to pray prayers of blessing and repentance over London (which linked with prayer meetings taking place in every other London borough on the same day). This meeting seemed catalytic for churches joining in unity and marked an acceleration in answers to prayer, opportunities to pray for those in authority and the forging of new relationships.

There was a rising tide of stabbings and street violence amongst the youth of South West London. A second civil service themed "Crime and Safety on the Streets" saw members of the council, Community Support Officers, schools and churches worshipping and praying for a breakthrough in this area. Plans are already underway to build on the success of these meetings using the ROC model of regular, community-engaging prayer gatherings bringing together those who are already working to see the transformation of Wandsworth with Christians who are praying and believing for it.

Prayernet regularly prayer-walks schools, churches, and other key locations in the town. One of their recent prayer walks focused on one of the more challenging estates in the borough where a faithful intercessor had been praying for her neighbours from her humble ground-floor flat. Young people have recently started gathering at her home, listening to stories of faith and praying together.

A local politician and a council member joined the Wandsworth Prayernet on a recent prayer walk outside a proposed lap dancing club to be opened in the town centre. This was featured in the local papers and drew in over 200 letters of protest against the club. We also prayed outside the council for wisdom and for Central Government to look again at the licensing laws.

As I have been writing this section an email has just come through from the Prayernet people saying:

> "The Council and Police have just agreed today to fund us £15,000 per year for 2 years to begin STREET PASTORS!!! YEEEEEH GOD!"

Isn't God amazing?

Guildford, Surrey

Ian Nicholson, who has lived and worked in Guildford for many years, tells us: "Transforming society is not a destination but a process and united prayer has been at the heart of that process in Guildford, Surrey, for twenty-five years. It has created an environment of real trust between leaders which has enabled inter-church initiatives to emerge. Encouragingly, in those twenty-five years there have been no major church fallouts or splits in the town."

From this foundation in the early 90s the churches held several joint prayer weeks in which the Lord clearly spoke that in Guildford there is only one Church – albeit with many different expressions and congregations. This was more than a slogan, it came over with force and impact. From that point, many leaders and churches were looking for ways to co-operate and support each other. Joint youth work, worship events, intercessory groups and training courses were developed and at one point, hundreds of local Christians knelt in prayer on the High Street on a Saturday morning as a mark of repentance for their proud and separatist attitude to their town.

Later in the 90s more focused "Sowing Seeds of Revival" prayer weeks gathered smaller groups from many churches to pray and intercede. The *Transformations* videos had been widely watched and there was a new level of ownership with leaders seeing themselves as responsible for pastoring the town and not just churches. There were encouraging signs of change, particularly in youth work. Eight years earlier there had been only one full-time Christian youth worker in the town and now there were over thirty with two thirds of them operating outside of churches working with schools, students, marginalised young people and on the streets. Alongside that, many church youth groups were now growing and much more positive. Working together had helped them to accomplish more than they could do in isolation.

The story of transformation has continued into the twenty-first century. There have been attempts to connect and affirm Christians in workplace spheres: health, business, education, leisure, youth, arts, politics, Church and family, alongside growing Church unity.

Certainly there are many encouragements that Guildford is being transformed as a result of prayer. Great friendships across all denominations, Christian student ministry, youth community projects, skate days, multiple expressions of prayer, ministry to overseas students, ministry at the festivals to spiritual seekers, the Besom ministry to the poorer in the town, homeless projects, detox initiatives, late night street ministry, prayer groups in most schools and Christian Unions placed in three secondary schools.

Alongside this, most of the joint prayer is now through multiple 24-7 prayer weeks, whether in shops, churches, university campuses, cafés or offices. In January 2008 they launched a 24-7 House of Prayer, which will fill a quarter of each year with non-stop prayer uniting Christians from across the churches. Ian says, "Guildford has a tendency to settle for the good and the nice rather than pursuing God's best and this focused prayer is key to keep moving forward."

Ipswich

Ipswich in Prayer was birthed during the summer of 2000 and officially launched as an initiative at a joint celebration on 8th October, 2000. The desire is that all Christians in Ipswich will become involved in prayer for the town. Liz Beaton, Ipswich in Prayer co-ordinator, shares her testimony here:

> "Until the Summer of 1999 I was a secondary school teacher at Ipswich High School. But during the early part of that year, God called me to come out of teaching. I knew He had a specific job for me to do, but that did not become clear until the summer of the following year. When the instruction to 'pray for Ipswich' did come, it could not have been clearer. The directions I have received during personal prayer times and in my many prayer times with church leaders throughout the town have been very definite and specific. So we are moving forward as we feel God is leading and already we are seeing positive things happening.
>
> Before the launch, one of the church leaders was given a picture as we prayed. They saw a powerhouse set in the middle of a circle which they took to represent the town. Around the perimeter of this circle, small fires were starting to light, fed from the powerhouse by pipes. The power was going back and forth in both directions through these pipes

and the sectors in between were starting to warm and glow as the fires caught alight.

We have received several specific words from God from the Bible. The text which we were given very strongly before the launch was 2 Chronicles 7:14. In the week prior to October 8th, this text was continually appearing from many different sources and directions. At our first Evening of Prayer we received a direct word from God which was, 'Behold, I have begun a great work.' This was confirmed over the following week.

Out of the prayer which takes many forms including a 24-7 prayer shield, prayer meetings, breakfast prayer meetings and special days of prayer, a vision for social action came to the churches. Groups were set up to help with addictions, eating disorders and other areas of social need, including 'town pastors', who patrol the streets to help those in need."

Scotland

In 2007 "Connecting Scotland"[15] took place from Easter to Pentecost when for fifty days teams of people walked and drove the length of Scotland covering some 5,000 miles, meeting and praying with local Christians en route. At the end of this they had met with eight thousand people and had handed out almost a quarter of a million "Father's Love letters". Leaders say, "We believe we have left behind a 'connectedness' in the Body of Christ that is continuing to bring God's people together in unity to make Scotland a place of commanded blessing."

In Glasgow, Steven and Helen Anderson have been running Prayer for the City[16] since December 1999 after leaving the pastoral care ministry where Steven was minister of Castlemilk Baptist Church. Small prayer meetings were held in the city centre on Friday evenings and leaders' prayer times began on the south side of the city. Out of these events the present ministry has grown. Through the Prayer for the

City ministry they seek to encourage vision for the transformation of the city, united believing, persevering prayer,
and prepare the Church to reap a harvest. One of the aims of
the ministry is to plant new churches and new expressions
of Church.

I went to speak to the church leaders' network in Glasgow
in November 2006. Leaders came from around Glasgow as
well as other parts of Scotland to hear about how prayer and
action work together. The churches in Glasgow have been
working together for years, running with lots of community
projects including things like FireStarters,[17] a youth action
project that mobilizes 120 young people in street evangelism
all across Scotland. In 2007 the focus has been on the east end
of Glasgow.

Strawberry Fields "Forprayer"

In October 2005 Gary and Dawn Lacey opened a Salvation
Army Boiler Room[18] in the wonderful Strawberry Fields
building in Liverpool, made famous by the Beatles' song. This
was to be a house of prayer which would use the 24-7 prayer
"boiler room" values to create a prayerful community which
would share its Gospel values by welcoming the poor and the
lost in for food and practical help as well as prayer.

In January 2004 I was invited to speak at the Salvation Army
Bible training college, William Booth College, in London. My
connections with the Salvation Army had been growing since
my visit to the conference they hold each May in Southport
called Roots. I have to admit feeling quite intimidated by the
surroundings, especially the huge portraits of Catherine and
William Booth behind me as I spoke. After the sermon we
started to pray. My Salvation Army friend, Jo Norton, crept up
behind me and whispered in my ear, "When are you going to
prophesy?" It shocked me a little and it was amusing. She had
heard me give prophetic words and assumed I would be doing
so on this occasion. I did not seem to be able to hear

prophetically that night, but her faith pushed me. The next thing I knew I was prophesying over a young man. I discovered later that it was Jo's son. I was moved to learn a few weeks ago that he still has the prophecy written on his bedroom wall. Next, the Holy Spirit seemed to draw my attention to a married couple and I told them that I felt they would work in a large urban city with the poor. Gary writes:

"Sitting in my workroom one night in our flat at William Booth College in London, where we were studying towards becoming Salvation Army ministers, God plainly gave me a vision to build a house of prayer in Liverpool, my home city.

Reading Isaiah 56 verse 7 I saw a massive place of prayer, healing, deliverance and restoration. I saw massive street outreach to the lost. I saw justice being pursued for the unloved. I saw an amazing prayer community developing. I shared the vision with my wife, Dawn, and a tutor at college called Phil Garnham, who told us, 'You need to plant a boiler room!' I didn't know much about 24/7 right then or indeed boiler rooms, so I went and met with our friend and prayer leader, Lyndall Bywater, who shared with us a prophetic word about building a house of prayer, and again we discussed boiler rooms. Also, Debra Green from Manchester shared a prophetic word almost identically matching Lyndall's word, so we kind of knew we had to follow what God was saying!

We were appointed when we were ordained and commissioned as Ministers to Liverpool where we were asked to plant a Salvation Army church in the south Liverpool area, a highly populated inner city area of Liverpool. We shared our vision with the Salvation Army Leadership in Liverpool who supported it totally and so we began to pray and connect with people over our first year. Working right from the start with the 24/7 SA prayer network, we began to look and pray into the Boiler room seriously, looking at the six core elements and seeing how we could shape the vision God gave us with those things in mind.

After nearly two years of praying, working and shaping what God was saying we were ready to look for a Boiler room building and Strawberry Field Children's Home, which presently belongs to the Salvation Army, became available after its closure this year, and God has amazingly given us this fantastic place to use until the Salvation Army make a decision on its future, which will take some time. So God said, 'Get in and launch the Boiler room and I will take care of the future.' We are now in and the prayer rooms are established. We have built a team of nine people over this year that God has just connected, each with gifts and skills that will be vital to the future of South Liverpool Boiler room at Strawberry Field."

The Daily Star reported in October 2005:

"For more than 40 years, the name *Strawberry Fields* has been synonymous with salvation. Now the historic building, immortalised by John Lennon's 1960s lyric, has undergone a spiritual re-birth of its own. Four months after closing its doors as a Salvation Army-run children's home, the site yesterday re-opened as a monastic-style refuge for religious contemplation. Known as the *Boiler Room*, the building has been revamped to house eight prayer rooms, including a multi-purpose meeting room, and a 'chill out' meditation room."

Strawberry Fields continues to house the prayer initiative and Gary and Dawn also lead a church there which has almost outgrown the main room. I have visited them on several occasions and have been totally inspired by their vision and faith.

Bell Farm: one congregation can make a difference

Bell Farm [19] is one of the many outer London housing estates built after the Second World War to accommodate former residents of the heavily bombed East End. In the centre of the estate the developers left a piece of land for a church and community centre. In the mid 1950s the Shaftesbury Society built a Gospel Hall on the land, and in late 1979 Tony Pilkington and his family moved to take up the leadership of Bell Farm Christian Centre.

In the 1990s juvenile crime began to increase significantly on the Bell Farm estate. With a population of four thousand, a group of local young people decided that the area would be "their patch" to dominate. They began harassing shopkeepers and intimidating local residents. Finally, it escalated in to violence. Young people prevented cars from driving down certain roads by standing on the roundabouts and jumping out in front of vehicles. They vandalised cars, set them on fire, threw bricks through house and church building windows and even made death threats.

The church community tried to resist the oppression; the Local Authority was lobbied and an Initiative Group aimed to find a response to the situation. But the church congregation began to recognise the spiritual battle occurring in the community and they began to pray.

Forty days of prayer and fasting were organised and in the weeks leading up to this, harassment and attacks were as strong as ever and the Police were frequently called. However, in the middle of the forty days, the attacks against the centre subsided. Tony Pilkington says, "Whereas before we could call the Police to the centre several times in one week, in the year following the prayer and fasting we only called them twice. After the forty days of prayer and fasting there was a really noticeable change in atmosphere. Whenever we used to return to the estate it was like there was a knot in your stomach, the oppression was almost smothering. There's no longer that feeling now."

As a specific answer to prayer, a Christian beat officer was appointed for the Bell Farm estate. "He became a tremendous support to us as a church, and to many of us individually," says Tony, "and this was so clearly a blessing from God. It provided a very important personal link with the local Police and the officer was able to support us in so many ways. We were also able to support the Police and we began to pray for them."

Prayer alongside action became a vital part of counteracting the intimidation. At one point a small group met every evening for a week to prayer walk around the road where the main gang members lived. On the final evening, four groups stood on the corners surrounding the road and prayed. As they left, some young people approached them and asked what they were doing. They shared that they were praying and the young people said, "Will you pray for us?"

Bell Farm Christian Centre became recognised by representatives from other agencies as having a role to play in responding to the needs of the local community. Tony comments, "Bell Farm Church was the only community building and group functioning on the estate." It was due to the strong reputation, relationships and respect that the Bell Farm community had built up at all levels, from local people to police officers and council executives.

What began as verbal abuse became sustained violence to people and property until ultimately the ring leaders were imprisoned and one family was evicted from the estate. The power of God through prayer has transformed this community.

Hope08: Importance of Prayer

When the vision for Hope08[20] began to grow, it became very evident that if the whole Church was to be mobilized for the whole nation for the whole year, reaching out with the Good News of Jesus in word and deed in 2008, all the preparation and planning and delivery would need to be steeped in prayer.

Hope08 was launched at a World Prayer Centre[21] Trumpet Call day of prayer and proclamation in October 2006 at the NEC in Birmingham and so began a year of prayer in 2007 and many individuals, churches, towns and cities took up the challenge to start praying ahead of Hope08. Jane Holloway, from the World Prayer Centre, is the prayer Director for Hope08. Jane was called by God to get involved in the emerging movement for prayer in 1993. Working first with Crosswinds and then with the Evangelical Alliance as Prayer Co-ordinator she was directed by a number of prophetic words to network the people that were being raised up in prayer leadership in towns, cities, counties and regions across the UK nationally. For her last two years at the EA she also took on the role as Evangelism Co-ordinator and was then able to network leaders involved in both prayer and evangelism. Currently she is National Prayer Director at the World Prayer Centre, Birmingham, and continues to encourage, network and mobilize prayer for mission and transformation.[22] Jane is passionate about helping the Church rediscover the centrality of prayer in its life and mission.

Greater Manchester and Greater London both ran 24-7 prayer unbroken from 1st January 2007 until 31st December 2007 with individuals and churches standing in the gap to pray for their communities and the nation. Neither city knew the other was planning this when they began! London is currently continuing with its "canopy of prayer",[23] linking with other centres around the UK.

2008 started with many prayer events and celebrations for old and young alike in churches, cathedrals and out on the streets. Prayer parties, prayer booths, 24-7 prayer and prayer services all took place and the Hope08 Prayer Declaration was prayed across the nation. The Hope08 *Great Ideas* book provides many creative ways to make prayer central in all that will be planned during the high points in 2008. Hope08 are encouraging all involved to join the prayer adventure and meet with others to pray in prayer triplets for friends who are not yet Christians between Easter and September.

The third Global Day of Prayer,[24] which takes place on Pentecost Sunday each year, will see many Christians in the UK stopping to pray and link with Christians in over 200 nations in the middle of Hope where you live in May 2008.

As I have been researching these stories from across the nation, which are only a sample of those we could have mentioned, I am reminded that prayer really works. One interesting factor to me though is how many times do we pray before it works and for how long? Matthew's Gospel reminds us to ask, seek and knock. In the New Living Translation, it reads, *'Keep on asking, and you will be given what you ask for. Keep on looking, and you will find. Keep on knocking, and the door will be opened'* (Matthew 7:7). Persistent prayer changes things, so don't give up too soon, you may be almost there.

Notes

1. www.tearfund.org/News/Latest+news/
   NEW+SURVEY+20+million+pray+in+the+UK.htm
2. www.24-7prayer.com
3. www.24-7prayer.com/cm/content/785
4. Dr J. Edwin Orr was born in Belfast in 1912 and concluded his work on earth in 1987. Professor Orr was passionately committed to Jesus Christ and dedicated his life to understanding and furthering the work of God, especially in revival and spiritual awakening. Dr Orr has much to say to the Christian world today, because his message was a profoundly powerful, eloquent, and accurate explanation of what the Bible says about revival, awakening and the deeper Christian life.
5. www.24-7prayer.com/cm/content/category/4
6. www.prayerweek.com
7. www.transformations-ireland.org
8. www.summermadness.co.uk
9. www.xpressionportadown.org
10. www.spark07.com

11. www.glolurgan.co.uk
12. www.ctj.org.je
13. www.onevoiceyork.org.uk – a charity which began in 1990 and is now an umbrella organisation for much of the Christian activity across York today.
14. www.globaldayofprayer.co.uk
15. www.connectingscotland.com
16. www.pftcglasgow.com
17. www.firestartersuk.org (see Chapter 10, "Beacons of Hope").
18. www.boiler-rooms.com/cm/boilerrooms/32
19. www.bfcc.org.uk; this story is written up in a book produced by Shaftesbury, *Lightening the Darkness*, available from www.shaftesburysociety.org
20. www.hope08.com
21. www.worldprayer.org.uk
22. A new website is now available providing prayer information, resources and links to all the prayer initiatives across British Isles and Ireland and globally; www.prayerforum.org
23. www.canopyofprayer.org
24. www.globaldayofprayer.co.uk

The Festival Model: in the UK

Festival fervour

I have been privileged to be part of two citywide festivals in Manchester in 2000 and 2003. Since then we've been hearing about festivals in villages, towns and cities across the UK on a regular basis.

In many ways the first of these, Soul-Survivor: The Message 2000 (sometimes shortened to Message 2000 or even SSM2K), became the template for the new festival model that has emerged in the UK over the last few years. It is hugely encouraging to see the inspiration it has been to so many people. I have heard reports of festivals in Merseyside, London, Brighton, Bristol, Glasgow, Devon, Chester, Preston and Newcastle. As well as these large city festivals, it is equally exciting to see festivals happening on a smaller scale in towns and villages.

SSM2K[1] took place in the summer of 2000 with two hundred partner churches from across the denominational spectrum. Eleven thousand people, the majority in their teens and early twenties, from around the UK and beyond volunteered weeks of holiday time. Proclamation evangelism and social action took place side-by-side, facilitated by youth organisations like Soul Survivor, The Message, Youth For Christ and Oasis. The activities engaged in were highly visible in the community and included community fun days, DIY projects, environmental initiatives, clean-up campaigns, sports programmes and activities for the elderly. Local churches worked together in a wonderful demonstration of Christian unity. Many crime hotspots were made safe again for the public and at the big evening events in the Manchester Evening News Arena, the city's main venue for high profile events, thousands gathered each night for evangelistic concerts at which hundreds responded to Jesus. It was a huge lesson learning that evangelism and social action are just sides of the same kingdom coin.

Festivals – a new model of mission

Matt Wilson, Director of Mission for The Message Trust,[2] has been at the forefront of pioneering the festival model in the UK. He writes:

> "Over the last few years, a new model of mission has emerged from the UK's big urban centres. Manchester, Liverpool, Newcastle and London have all hosted major initiatives. God seems to have been directing individuals by His Holy Spirit. The fingerprints of Jesus clearly characterize this convergence of words and action, this holistic new Gospel model.
>
> It's incredibly exciting to know that without great fuss and fanfare communities throughout the nation have been experiencing God's love. Worthy of special mention is the way churches have been connecting in new ways with statutory agencies such as the Police, local councils, Social Services and community workers. This is perhaps one of the most important objectives of the festival model – to build bridges and make an impact relationally with the secular authorities who share our language of renewal.
>
> For about two years now conversations have been taking place behind the scenes, leaders have been discussing the

festival model and asking: 'Is God doing a new thing in the nation? Can it be that God is raising the spiritual temperature? Is He opening a new door of opportunity for His people?' The answer has been a resounding yes! So now is the time to ask yourself: how could we implement the festival model in our region?"

Festival Manchester – the inspiration

In 2001 I was part of a group of Brits who were invited to visit a Luis Palau Festival in Santa Cruz, California (somebody had to go!) Liz Biddulph from Soul Survivor,[3] Matt Wilson and I were amongst a group who saw the festival first hand. Over 100,000 people gathered in Santa Cruz for "Beachfest" (more about this in the next chapter), an event that was to have a huge impact on our lives and which became a real inspiration for what was about to happen in the UK.

Around the same time, Andy Hawthorne, CEO of The Message Trust, and the Luis Palau Evangelistic Association team were meeting to discuss a large scale festival, combining the big USA party model with the "on the streets" social action model pioneered in Manchester in 2000. We have no beach in Manchester, but we do have plenty of parks, so the vision was birthed: Festival Manchester: on the streets/in the park.

In 2002 Andy Hawthorne asked me to work full time on Festival Manchester organising teams as the person responsible for church liaison and prayer co-ordination. For twelve months I travelled the North-West recruiting partner churches, over five hundred in all, from different denominations and streams. In the summer of 2003 it seemed as though all the hard work was finally realised. Here are some of the highlights from the Festival report:

> A radical "celebration of faith, hope and life" came to a grand finale as Festival Manchester drew a crowd of over thirty thousand people to enjoy Christian music, extreme sports and

family fun in the city's famed Heaton Park in September 2003. The event brought to a successful close one of the largest Christian events ever staged in the UK.

The US-based Luis Palau Evangelistic Association and Manchester's Message Trust partnered with over five hundred churches, the Manchester and Salford City Councils, Greater Manchester Police, and dozens of corporate and private supporters to produce the event, which combined community service and social action projects with a massive music festival.

Close to five thousand volunteer/delegates from throughout the UK and Western Europe worked on over three hundred service projects in some of the city's most deprived areas. Over four days, some seventy five thousand hours of work were contributed to the cleanup, repair and upgrading of public and private facilities in dozens of estates.

On the weekend, the volunteers joined an estimated two-day crowd of more than fifty-five thousand who came to the park to enjoy major Christian music artists like Toby Mac, Tait, The Tribe, and the London Community Gospel Choir, along with a variety of festival activities. There was a Kidz Zone play area, vintage and extreme car show and a custom-built, ten thousand square foot Skate Park featuring some of the world's top skateboard and BMX professionals. World evangelist and author Luis Palau shared the message of good news and hope, which he has presented in over seventy countries in front of eighteen million people.

"This festival showed the city and the region that followers of Jesus are joyful and selfless," said Palau. "The dedicated service of the volunteers ... the cooperation of the churches and local agencies ... the lives that were eternally changed ... it all came together this week under God in Manchester."

Festival: Manchester will leave a lasting mark on the city, from the hundreds of new believers who made decisions for Christ during the week to the massive Skate Park, built by volunteers with donated materials, which will soon be permanently installed at a Manchester recreation facility.

"The full impact of the festival will only be known in Heaven," said Andy Hawthorne. "We've dreamt of a Church community that's not only for the like-minded, but one that gets involved with broken communities that desperately need Jesus. At Festival: Manchester that dream started to become a reality."

Over fifteen hundred recorded decisions for Christ were made in the streets and in the park during the festival.

Do Festivals work?

A couple of years ago a lady from the South of England rang me. Her son had been a volunteer at Message 2000. He worked on one of the social action projects on a tough Salford council estate called "The Valley", alongside nine hundred and ninety nine other young volunteers, (including my own daughter Becky). The lady explained that her son had loved his experience in Manchester, but had since gone off to university and had become quite disillusioned. She wanted to know if I could tell her if anything which might encourage her son. Had his work been worthwhile?

"Do festivals really work?" she asked. She wondered if they had a lasting impact. We had said quite boldly, "no more hit and run". Was this really the case?

I was able to tell her that several years after Message 2000, Swinton Valley was a better place to live. A vibrant local church had been planted, a community resource centre established and there was now a waiting list for homes on the estate as crime had been so significantly reduced.

Her question got me thinking though. "There is still a long way to go and many challenges ahead," I thought. However, in the last year I have heard two amazing stories which fill me with hope and awe at what God can do through festivals. The first of these stories comes from Bob Collier in his own words. Bob serves as a police officer with Greater Manchester Police. In 1999, he left his job working as a Community Police Officer on the Valley Estate in Swinton, for a job as a divisional Youth Development Officer in the Salford division. Here's his story:

> "In the year 2000, I received a totally unexpected phone call from a colleague and now very close personal friend of mine, Phil Gleave, who at the time was working at Greater Manchester Police headquarters. Phil told me that 'The Message Trust' had arranged a gathering of over twenty thousand Christians from all over the world to meet in Manchester to make a difference, but that they still needed to find work for one thousand Christians who would be arriving in five weeks time.
>
> I had contacts from my days as a Community Police Officer and I sent them to the Valley Estate in Swinton.
>
> There was no doubt that the phone call began to make a huge fundamental difference in my life, both with the work I would have to do and the impact meeting these people would have on my personal life. In partnership with the 'Message 2000' and Salford city council, we seized the opportunity to undertake the most ambitious 'Make A Difference'[4] project to date."

"Operation Valley", based on a residents' wish-list, saw two hundred and ten tons of rubbish removed from the estate, eighty residents' gardens improved, a community garden (which is still in great condition thanks to new local gardening groups that have since come into being) and an outdoor amphitheatre created (which drama groups still enjoy using). This work was completed in February 2001. The volunteer teams also improved the community centre and secured toys and equipment for pre-school kids.

A linear park was created, vehicle access improved and a dog walking area created. The Valley resource centre saw a new wall built at the front of the premises, a restructured rear yard, access gate, redecoration, carpet for hall and stairs, widening for disabled access and many more features.

In addition to these items, graffiti was removed from the community centre, resource centre, the two substations, the boulders in the car park and from various locations around the estate.

Months later crime statistics showed a reduction in crime on the Valley Estate of 45%. This was a spectacular decrease and residents were reporting that an unprecedented "feel good factor" had emerged on their estate. Jack Straw, from the Home Office, was so impressed he visited the estate to see the transformation for himself and was greatly impressed.

Bob says that there were a number of factors that he just could not explain (we call them miracles, but at this stage in his personal journey, he was not so familiar with our language!): how the finances of £500,000 were provided in just a few months (although a chunk of that was donated by the Police from their crime reduction budget – the first and only example of which I am aware of the Police sponsoring evangelism with cash!); how the criminal element suddenly stopped causing trouble and instead began to pitch in and help with the projects; how a chance visit to ASDA secured free bread and fillings to feed one thousand people every day (plus Coca Cola and Golden Wonder Crisps).

"Every day for ten days I would hand out spades, litter picks, bin bags, wheelbarrows, rakes, and hoes to these young volunteers and ask them to go into the back of a garden of dense undergrowth that hadn't seen the light of day for years. These young volunteers would greet me with a smile and thank me for all I was doing and for allowing them to serve the community. They would go about their given task with a spring in their step and usually singing."

At the final evening gathering at the MEN Arena, Phil Gleave, Chief Superintendent Chris Wells and Bob received a loving and warm welcome. On the same evening a donation from the residents of the Valley Estate was handed over to the organisers of Message 2000.

> "This was an estate with high unemployment, single parent families, with high deprivation scores and yet they had so much love, gratitude and respect in their hearts for the work everyone had put in on their behalf they felt moved to contribute what little they had. All of the above along with the many more personal encounters I had with people participating caused me to stop and ask myself one simple question: 'What have these people got that I haven't?'
>
> In August 2001 I played a part in coordinating a second Valley-style project '2K1 The Urban Adventure'. The results were again astonishing and here is a quote from a local resident, which appeared in the *Manchester Evening News*:

> 'The much-maligned Police and council came together to work the biggest success to date, with the Christian Festival, encamped in Buile Hill Park. Apart from the practical labours, they brought an atmosphere of normality not seen in 30 years. Gone from the park were the young, sullen, hostile faces of our usual park youth, replaced by bright, smiling faces you associate with the normal young.
>
> Many thanks to all concerned. It was so positive.'

In 2003 Festival: Manchester brought me back into close working contact with my friend Phil Gleave. As by this time I had seen so many young and mature Christians complete the most incredible tasks against all the odds, now was the time I needed to find out more.

I made Phil aware of my mission and he invited me along to his church. I took him up on his offer the following Sunday and two members of the 'Welcome Team' embraced me as their long lost friend when they greeted me in the reception area. I felt like I'd begun my journey in the right place. Within a very short space of time I was enrolled on a 'Christianity Explored' course.

With regular attendance at church, Home Group and various courses, my life suddenly began to change and slowly but surely I was able to see where I had gone wrong. Then one evening in the summer of 2005, faced with the unquestionable truth that Jesus died on the cross to forgive us our sins, I knelt and asked God for forgiveness and became a Christian.

On the 6th of May 2006 I was baptised and this particular evening was made even more special as my partner Debbie unexpectedly gave her life to our Saviour. All of a sudden my life, both private and work based, was being lived to the full, as a Christian family working how we felt God would want us to. Then on the 9th of June 2007 Debbie and our little girl Grace took the next logical step in their walk of faith and were baptised.

Finally, on Saturday the 4th of August 2007, my friend, colleague and Minister of my church, Phil Gleave, conducted the wedding ceremony between Debbie and me."

Bob's story is so moving and such an encouragement to us all, it reminds us of both the urgency to pray for our Police force and the value of working together with secular agencies for the good of the community.

Swinton Valley today – the dream lives on

The second story tells us more about what the Valley Estate is like today, seven years on from SSM2K.

Ruth Lacey is the team leader for Eden Swinton and has been part of a team working with the Swinton Valley community since Message 2000. Ruth and her team are part of The Message Trust initiative Eden, which organises volunteers and full-time team leaders to live and work in the most challenging parts of Greater Manchester. Their goal is to build relationships in the community over a long period of time. In 2007, Ruth and her Eden team, organised another week long initiative, albeit on a smaller scale than the festival, to make a further impact on their community: Valley Pride Week sought to restore to the community pride for their area (historic reputations can be tough to change) and bring a spirit of fun and celebration to the people living there. This was a week to bring God's goodness into people's lives through living the life, having fun, serving and sharing with others. It is in this real life way that communities are impacted and changed.

Despite many groups, including the local council, telling the main steering group that the week was "too ambitious" and simply too much work for volunteer groups to achieve, they were proven wrong by the success of Valley Pride Week. Afterwards they came back with nothing but praise for the organisers.

Throughout the week there were a variety of activities: a football competition, a fun run, a community clean-up and a climbing wall. In the evenings, numerous events were organised for all ages, such as a ladies night and a family film night. After much prayer on the issue, during the opening ceremony the sun shone brightly as the community noticed grey skies all around the outside of the estate, with not a cloud in the area immediately above their heads!

Throughout the week the sun continued to shine brightly and not a drop of rain fell for the entire six days! One evening the Eden team fed over seventy hungry people with an "all you can eat" Chinese meal. Everyone ate several plates each and there was plenty left over and at a cost of only £62. Indeed, some of those who were fed genuinely believed that God must have multiplied the food!

To the surprise (and almost concern) of the Eden team, some of the "hardest to reach" women in the area came along to the Ladies Night. Most of these women have suffered terribly throughout their lives with abuse, neglect and mistreatment. For many this has made some of them hard, bitter and very angry people while others were just totally broken. Throughout the beauty and pampering evening the team had conversations with people they had previously found few opportunities to talk to. Massive barriers were broken down that evening and the team found themselves talking deeply and personally and laughing hysterically with a group of women they now call friends.

> Do festivals work? I hope the lady who rang me a few years ago is reading this book. If you are, please tell your son "thank you" for playing a part in what God is doing today in Swinton Valley.

Merseyfest

The cities of Manchester and Liverpool have been intention-ally working together since the visit in 1996 of Argentinian Evangelist, Ed Silvoso. Ed had been invited to come to Manchester to speak at a conference and had said that he would only come if two cities linked. The remarkable way this actually happened is a story in itself[5] but the bottom line is that leaders of churches from Manchester and Liverpool (cities previously known as arch rivals in many ways) got together and organised a prayer gathering to join forces in praying for the region. A partnership emerged which would prove invaluable for the festivals which were to follow many years later. We have discovered, over and over again, the value of partnership when it comes to successful festivals and community projects.

The vision for Merseyfest came out of a meeting between Andy Hawthorne and the leaders' network in Liverpool "Together for the Harvest". Andy asked the Merseyside churches to support Festival:Manchester, planned for August 2003. Despite the history of antipathy between the two cities, God had been knitting our hearts together since the joint prayer meeting back in 1996. The leaders responded enthusiastically to Andy's request and began to promote and publicise what would previously have looked like a rival event. In the end, 1,000 delegates came from Merseyside to participate in Festival:Manchester. In Manchester we were blown away by their service and generosity. They saw first hand what God can do through a large scale, citywide festival and returned to Liverpool with fresh vision and faith. John Cavanagh, from Together for the Harvest, writes: "A prayer meeting of Merseyside leaders was called and we asked the question, 'Why not here?' It spoke into the passion of our hearts to see our community transformed, and in prayer we believed God confirmed to us that we should do it."

And Merseyfest was born. Described by local leaders as a movement for change; ordinary people from all walks of life working together to change their community for good.

Project Director Mike Kerry says, "Since we began, there have been hundreds of projects of kindness bringing positive change throughout the region. We have helped scores of communities work together to improve their environment, hold concerts and kid's events and we even put together a massive Festival attended by 75,000 people!"

Merseyfest 2005 was a week long event in August 2005, split into two parts: community projects and a weekend event (following Manchester's "On the Streets/In the Park" model). Thousands of people from the region, across the UK and the globe came to Liverpool to make Merseyside safer, stronger, cleaner and kinder. Merseyfest threw a massive, free weekend event at Liverpool's Croxteth Park. Featuring bands, DJs, live MCs, breakdancers, Europe's largest outdoor skate park, bungee jumping, urban arts, a massive firework display, a family interactive zone with bouncy castles, games, face painting and robotic.

In all, forty-nine church-driven community projects took place across the region under the vision: "Change Communities for Good". Christians from all across the region stepped out of their comfort zones and rolled up their sleeves in partnership with other organisations and made a real difference in their communities.

Churches in Merseyside are building on the good work achieved by Merseyfest and are busy planning Festival of Hope,[6] a unique coming together of three events from 4th–14th June 2008. The culmination will be on Saturday 14th June with a huge Gospel Arts street party in Hope Street, Liverpool. The three major events are an exciting contribution to the Capital of Culture year. Merseyfest is a key partner in delivering "Festival of Hope 08" along with LJM Group and Liverpool Hope University. The vision is to make a significant and lasting Christian contribution to the Capital of Culture year. Liverpool Hope University is expecting two thousand delegates to attend their Global Youth congress "The Big Hope".[7] Merseyfest will look to work with many of the international delegates by involving them in Merseyfest projects during June 08.

Observing the effects of two cities, Manchester and Liverpool, inspiring and influencing each other had a profound effect on me. I recalled a verse I had read some months ago:

"This is what the LORD *Almighty says: 'Many peoples and the inhabitants of many cities will yet come, and the inhabitants of one*

city will go to another and say, "Let us go at once to entreat the
LORD and seek the LORD Almighty. I myself am going." ' "
(Zechariah 8:20–21)

Following Festival:Manchester I received a number of telephone calls and emails from Christians outside the North-
West requesting my help and advice. I felt sure that God was
speaking to me about learning from and building on these
principles of united prayer and action and so (another long
story that's told in *City-Changing Prayer*), in September 2003 I
set up the charitable trust City Links, which I still direct today.
Our aim is to foster, forge and further unity between cities
across the UK and abroad for the sake of effective mission and
transformation.[8]

Soul in the City – London
From 26th July to 6th August 2004, over 20,000 Christians
from across the UK gathered in London to take part in
hundreds of community projects and demonstrate that
"actions speaker louder than words". 11,663 young people
and 9,500 local churchgoers worked together in a mission that
both proclaimed and demonstrated the Gospel to Londoners
regardless of background.

London was sliced into seven areas, each with a hosting
church leader, who would then recruit local churches to
work together in devising projects which would improve the
quality of life for local residents. Churches that signed up
would be supplied with teams of young people working
with congregation members to get jobs done. Projects
were developed to assist churches in their efforts at serving
and impacting their local communities so that they would
be sustainable and continue once the visiting delegates
left.

St Paul's Cathedral hosted J. John, a well known evangelist,
who over the ten nights of the mission used the Ten

Commandments to speak of the relevance of the Gospel. 1,200 people made first time commitments to God during these events!

On the final day, fifteen thousand people came together at Trafalgar Square for an open-air celebration of the Christian faith, expressing the commitment of the churches of London to continue to serve their neighbours.

The sense of community built by the projects brought together a mass of London residents. Many left saying, "We haven't seen anything like this before" and "When can we do it again?" And perhaps most importantly, church leaders were left open-mouthed, saying, "We can't go back to doing things on our own." Having discovered and worked with neighbouring churches, lasting alliances have been made and now Soul in the City – London continues as an independent collective of the mission's partner churches.

A month after the festival, Dave Vann, then Public Relations Officer of Oasis Trust, visited a council estate in Ealing to find out whether Soul in the City could bring about lasting change in one of West London's most notorious neighbourhoods. Here are his comments:

"Walking around the Greenman Lane housing estate, just off West Ealing's high street, it is easy to see why local churches should choose to send two hundred and fifty volunteers to the area as part of the Soul in the City initiative.

Families live in fear of the gangs who have made drugs, crime and anti-social behaviour a part of their daily routine on the estate. A week before my visit to the estate, Police had been called out on three separate occasions to deal with incidents of violent crime.

The most visible sign that things have changed since enthusiastic young Christians invaded the estate one month ago, is the large mural that now adorns the wall of the main car park. The bright colours of the painting, which depicts scenes of children playing together, stand in stark contrast to the greyness of the surrounding buildings.

'We had such a tremendous response from the local residents,' explains Heidi Abrahams, a twenty-five year old youth worker from the Ealing Christian Centre who helped co-ordinate the Soul in the City work on the estate. 'People who had never previously opened their doors to strangers were throwing them open and inviting us in for food and drinks.'

At a meeting of the Greenman Lane Residents' Association, several mothers from the estate recall with excitement the work undertaken by the white-shirted group of Christians during the two-week initiative. Painting walls, clearing rubbish, cleaning hallways, planting flowerbeds, befriending the elderly, renovating a community centre – the list is long and varied. In addition, many people from the estate attended the 'Friday Festivals', which provided food and entertainment in the nearby park, and the evening music events staged at the Ealing Christian Centre.

According to Linda, the Chair of the Residents' Association, 'Soul in the City really cleaned the place up and people feel a lot better about the estate now than they did before.' Another resident, mother of one Lisa, was pleased that the volunteers were able to give children on the estate something to do during the two weeks.

During the two weeks, Police reported having to make no call outs to the estate, with residents also noting that no incidents of violent crime had taken place during the same period. In addition, residents were pleased to see less drug-taking on the estate while the volunteers were working on the estate."

Love Bristol Festival

Love Bristol[9] Festival was an initiative of the Bristol church community to recruit hundreds of people from the Bristol region and give 20,000 hours of community action on the streets of south Bristol, as an expression of love and care for the communities. Over one hundred projects proposed by the local community were completed by more than seven hundred and fifty enthusiastic volunteers. These included murals, decorating schools, church halls, community buildings, garden clear ups, litter picking, music workshops, sports coaching, extreme sports competitions, graffiti removal, holiday clubs and community fun days.

"To see these young people freely giving their time and doing so happily and unselfishly was very special. The best thing was the knowledge that groups of wonderful people were spread out over our lovely city, making it better," said the leader of Arnos Vale Residency Committee. Around ten thousand people visited the festival site at Hengrove Park over the course of the five day event and about six thousand people attended the Sunday Festival day.

One of the stories that came back from the event includes the testimony of a young delegate called Med, who had come in a complex state and not close to God at all. Med was prayed for during the festival and God subsequently moved in his life to comfort some of the heavy things on his heart. Med was moved to give his life to God. One of the men who had prayed for him brought him to church after the festival had finished and Med is now a key member of his house group and sharing a house with another Christian lad.

As a result of the project eighty young people returned in October to carry out more community projects in partnership with south Bristol groups and agencies, and twenty Bristol University students have worked with a local youth worker to carry out projects in Hartcliffe. The South Bristol Church community, of all denominations, has established a coalition to work with the council and the Bristol Partnership, and has been invited to work with the South Bristol C21 group (funded by Bristol City Council, EP and South West Regional Development Agency).

Journalist Heather McKay reviewed the festival for the BBC:

> "The *Love Bristol Festival* attracted many people of different ages and races who shared one thing in common, and that was not necessarily their religion. It was a genuine desire to help a community that they were proud to be a part of, in whatever way they were able."

Soul by the Sea

Brighton hosted their own festival, Soul by the Sea, in 2006. Local Christians were amazed at the level of inter-church cooperation that brought it into being. Nobody could remember anything remotely like it in living memory and someone described it as an ecumenical miracle. One of the measurable outcomes was that one hundred people came forward after J. John's talk to find out more about Christianity. More than sixty of these made a first-time confession of faith at this event. The consensus among the organisers was that this would be the first of many events under the Soul by the Sea banner.

In November 2007, I was invited to speak at the Brighton Evangelical Alliance (BEA made up of about twenty-five churches and four Christian organisations in the Brighton and Hove area).[10] Andy Au, who leads City Gate Church and has been in Brighton for over twenty-five years, is currently the Chairman. The group of church leaders meet twice a year for a retreat, as well as regularly to pray together. They are growing in friendship and mutual trust and support is blossoming. This relational network of church leaders is typical in many of our UK cities and towns. It provides a crucial foundation for the festival model.

I spoke about how prayer had been a real catalyst for effective mission in Manchester and that many other towns and cities have been discovering the power of united prayer. There was a fresh hunger in the meeting to see prayer as an urgent priority. I met two prayer warriors, Chris Leage, now aged eighty-two and her prayer partner Maisie Woodward, who have been praying for Brighton for decades. It was wonderful to see how encouraged they were by the response of the church leaders. Steve Walford from Christ the King Church spoke of his vision to see churches working together for the greater good of Brighton. This church already has an impressive track record with social action projects through their "Urban Impact" initiative.

David Treneer, pastor of Holland Road Church, spoke of his vision for the churches to work together for a beach festival in July 2008. One of the council leaders had even offered to give them a place on the sea front free of charge! The church has been meeting to pray for the Police and have recently made some good contacts.

Others spoke highly of projects like "Off the Fence"[11] which was started by Paul Young to minister to needy people in the Brighton and Hove region. The charity provides vital services to the most vulnerable and marginalised in the community, working in four areas: street homelessness, women at risk, education and providing supported accommodation for vulnerable young people.

Everyone agreed that 2008 presented the Church with an amazing opportunity to work with the local council and Police for the good of the city. The leaders were excited about the "Truth, Lies and Spies" event planned for January 2008 at the Brighton Dome. Future events are intended to be staged at larger venues and there is a vision for an open-air festival style event, perhaps to tie in with the celebration of "Hope" in 2008. "We're here for the long haul," Andy Au concluded. It seems that the Soul by the Sea festival is still alive and well.

Chesterfest

The vision for Chesterfest is for a continual, never-ending lifestyle of activity which will revolve around a central

"Summer Celebration Week" in July. A free, citywide week of music, teaching, festivities and community acts of kindness, culminating with a free Fun Day on a Sunday, currently enjoyed annually by over six thousand people.

Chesterfest is a citywide initiative which grew out of the smaller, more localized Hoolefest, an annual, week-long mission which works with local people, public services and the Police to develop a safer community and transform lives.

Andy Glover writes, "In 2007 our summer celebration week had twenty-one church partners, plus organisations who partnered with us including Christian and public sector bodies. We had one hundred and fifty youth involved, all from Chester, plus forty youth leaders. We ran twenty four CAKE (Community Acts of Kindness Experience) projects. We held evening outreach events and a 'Youth Events at the Cathedral' with the band Yfriday as the main act which attracted over five hundred young people. The Fun Day this year had over nine thousand visitors and over three hundred volunteers involved staffing all the activities."

Working with Chesterfest is Chester based initiative The Light Project,[12] which exists to actively demonstrate the Christian message in a relevant way and to equip others to do the same. Through The Light Project's youth groups, community work and schools' work, they have contact with over fourteen thousand children and young people every week. As well as taking drama and entertainment to the streets of Chester and working with Chester's homeless.

Like most of these festivals, Chesterfest is bathed in the kind of united prayer that many people say is the key to their success. The organisers include a Prayer Coordinator and most of the twenty-one partner churches have appointed specific "prayer reps" who communicate and meet together regularly and organise dynamic, inter-church prayer gatherings throughout the build up to the main event.

One exciting outcome is that their efforts have been appreciated not only by Christians and a few locals who have benefited from the action projects, but even by the media. The *Chester Chronicle* nominated Chesterfest "Team of the Year 2007" in a competition they ran called, "Your Champions Team of the Year".

Michael Green, Deputy Editor, said of the Chesterfest nomination for Your Champions: "There is nothing that we've seen throughout the year that fulfils the criteria of 'Your Champions' more than Chesterfest does. 'Your Champions' sets out to highlight the achievements of community action and the efforts of individuals and teams above and beyond the call of duty for the benefit of the local community. Chesterfest's efforts touched so many different parts of the community as well as galvanising the efforts of young people, while benefiting them too. Chesterfest was organised on such a huge scale with great ambition which didn't fall by the wayside. It achieved everything it set out to achieve and more – a 100% success."

The relationship with the City Council Area Committee has been strengthened as they have seen the sustainability and success of the Fun Day and Hoolefest/Chesterfest. A strong partnership was developed with the Cheshire Fire and Rescue Service who led a CAKE project and provided an activity at the Fun Day that they staffed. Phil Nicholls of the Fire and Rescue Service commented, "I just wanted to say thank you for the opportunity to get involved with Chesterfest. It was amazing to be a part of such a fantastic occasion ... What an example to the people of Chester. I have come away from the week really humbled by your commitment to serve the community. Thanks for letting me be a part of it!"

Isn't it brilliant when the Church makes such an impact that the pillars of the community are moved to voice their appreciation?

NE1[13] *(Newcastle and North-East)*

(Do you get it? NE1? ... Anyone ... Good, isn't it? But I have to admit it took me a while!)

This is another hugely successful festival based on lots of prayer and cross-church cooperation. The sort of thing that we're starting to take for granted but, say, ten or so years ago, would never have happened.

Here's the history: six years ago with encouragement from the Evangelical Alliance and the example of what God was doing in many cities of the UK, the leaders of "Together in Christ in Tyneside" mandated Robert Ward to seek God's will for a prayer strategy for our region. Under his leadership a steering group for a prayer network started to meet to pray and plan and listen to God.

By the end of 2002, Pray4Tyneside was birthed. Jenny Steiner, a member of the steering group, sensed God's call to her to coordinate and administer the network with Robert Ward as chairman.

Jenny explains, "Our aim was to see the region transformed to the glory of God, by the power of the risen Christ, by the raising up of an army of prayer watchmen and warriors, aware of the spiritual battle, seeking for God's mercy to rid the region of evil through:

- The blessing of God on His Church in repentance, unity and revival
- Increased evangelism
- The strengthening, protection and anointing of spiritual leadership in the area
- The establishment of righteous secular leadership.

"Praying for church unity – in particular the Together in Christ Group of leaders – is always a priority," she says. "We had a reconciliation walk across the eight bridges, praying for peace and reconciliation between Newcastle and Gateshead in the middle of the Millennium Bridge. We had a prayer cruise for one hundred and eighty people up and down to the mouth of the River Tyne, pouring wine onto the waters and having communion together as well as mighty prayers which bounced off the banks of the river. We have prayed over the city walls and gates."

As a result of the existing unity of the churches and established prayer networks like Pray4tyneside, the early stage foundations for the NE1 festival were laid. Jon Burns, Phil Glover and Ken Riley, the Directors of NE1 talk about their experience with their festival and give us some insight in to the impact it had on the region:

"During the twenty four months of preparation for NE1 we were thrilled at the number of churches that engaged with us in this bold mission partnership!

- Two hundred local churches across the North East had decided to partner with us.
- Wider partnerships with local councils and the Police were also operating in many locations as well at the central site at Herrington Country Park.
- The Bishop of Durham, Rt Rev. Tom Wright, committed to the project as our patron!

On Sunday 23 July over one thousand delegates arrived. The whole event started with a commissioning service where over four thousand people from the local churches joined our Bishop Tom for the evening. Rarely has there been such a gathering of adults and young people for worship in our region.

During the week itself three thousand volunteers were transported daily to one hundred and five local community projects – demonstrating God's love in a whole host of ways including clean up, sports outreach and youth café projects. The stories coming back of the impact being made through these acts of kindness are way beyond what we had hoped for and many areas are expressing an ongoing desire for further action. The sight of all our delegates leaving daily on thirty coaches and returning at the end of the day, tired but elated, will stay with us for a long time.

Our estimate is that over ten thousand young people attended over fifty high quality youth outreach events held in the evenings in twenty towns around the North East – over three thousand of whom came to the Big Top at Herrington Country Park on the Friday evening. Hundreds of young people responded to the opportunity to look further into the Christian message.

With over one hundred locations and fifty events, we are only just beginning to get some understanding of the real impact being made. On a daily basis we are receiving great stories of transformed communities and lives. One Whitley Bay team member reported, 'Having been challenged by a very aggressive lad when I was refereeing a football match, I was surprised to see him go forward at the end of the evening event in response to Mark Ritchie. I gently asked him if he knew what the queue was for. 'To meet Jesus,' he replied without hesitation! I felt two inches high for my lack of faith.' Thirty young people came forward to receive Christ as their Saviour that night.

Team after team reported young people were becoming Christians at the evening events throughout the week. Throughout the region for three nights of that week there were twenty events running each night. On the final Friday, four thousand young people were taken by coach to the NE1 campsite at Penshaw, near Durham, for a final evening event and many hundreds stood to make a commitment. Throughout the week about one thousand young people became Christians.

There is a feeling that the Church in the region has been re-energized for community involvement through this stimulating event.''

Impact:Preston – "on a smaller scale"

Andy Prosser, Project Coordinator for Impact:Preston, talks about their festival model, which, though on a smaller scale than the festivals in Manchester, Liverpool, Bristol, London and Newcastle, has the same values of community restoration at its heart and is founded on the same principles of prayer and radical, inter-denominational teamwork. "Festivals build community and friendship," he says. "By bringing churches and youth groups together they also build unity. Impact:Preston[14] was a programme of training, community engagement and social action that took place over nine days in the August of 2006. It was organised by a team of volunteers from churches across Preston and South Ribble in Lancashire."

Here is an extract from their report:

"What delighted my heart was to see God's kingdom values expressed in such practical ways:

- Every second of the three thousand eight hundred hours of service was given for free
- All the seven hundred burgers, eight hundred sausages and gallons of juice, tea and coffee were free
- Streets were cleaner (seventy odd bin bags cleaner), railings were painted (one hundred and ten meters), weeds were history, a community garden was well on the way
- Over one hundred and forty kids were entertained, families learned about fire safety and crime prevention, the elderly had a free lunch, twenty five families' clothes were ironed, individuals were trained in first aid
- Teenagers were entertained, kids improved their skating skills and over five hundred people had fun across two family fun days

One thing is clear to me, that Impact:Preston was a success. Many of the volunteers I have spoken to not only enjoyed serving the community, but expressed their desire to do something again. For me personally, it was a thousand small encounters that made the week worthwhile. It was the way that we engaged with the community *and* the way the community engaged with us. The Police, the council, the probation service, local businesses, local residents, and people who travelled in from surrounding towns, all played a part in building, as well as experiencing, community."

Summer Madness – Belfast

Summer Madness[15] was started by the Church of Ireland Youth Department twenty-one years ago. Its vision is simple: to help people catch the passion of Jesus and in doing so equip and empower them to take that passion and use it in their daily lives. It's Ireland's biggest Christian festival with over five thousand people coming together for five to seven days.

Christianity is not a static, inward looking faith, it is a dynamic and relevant reflection of the love of Jesus made real to us and to those around us. Summer Madness wants to create a festival that highlights and celebrates this. From worship and teaching from some of the best in Ireland and beyond, to gigs and jigs with some of the loudest and craziest bands about.

In 2003 Summer Madness added a brand new dimension to its programme. Just like the other towns and cities we've already seen, church leaders here were tuning into God's heart for community redemption and boldly launched "StreetReach" as an opportunity for people to put their faith into action in a real and simple way. In the first year one hundred and fifty people stayed for four days after Summer Madness to serve and bless the Lower Shankhill area in a variety of different ways – from cleaning streets to weeding gardens to playing football with kids in the park. In 2007 thousands of young people stayed for over a week serving nearly forty different communities in Belfast to show them the practical love of God. They said, "For us it's what being a Christian is all about and we want to challenge and equip people to be part of it."

Every summer in the lead up to 12th July, known in Northern Ireland as the "marching season", StreetReach moves bravely and powerfully into the toughest parts of the city to work alongside local community groups and churches. The organisers believe that the transformation of the community on the outside will lead to a transformation of the internal realm, that is, in how people view themselves and the communities they live in. StreetReach seeks to make people who are in various ways "on the edge" of our communities feel valued and included by showing them the radical love of Jesus in practical ways and earning the right to proclaim the Gospel in words when the time is right for each individual.

Find out what's breaking God's heart

It's thrilling to hear all these testimonies from towns and cities around the UK and very encouraging to see the common factors recurring in every case: not-yet-Christians saying positive things about the Church and softening in their attitudes to God, the physical environment of local communities being improved and local people taking increased responsibility to maintain the improvements, young people demonstrating enormous enthusiasm for projects that add credibility to their personal testimony of faith in Jesus Christ, and so on. We must remember, though, that at the heart of it all is prayer: that humbling of ourselves before the Lord so that His agenda is allowed to gain access to our hearts. Someone once preached, "Find out what's breaking God's heart and allow it to break yours as well" and that really is the key to redeeming our communities. And it's not just prayer as we know it – a little huddle of faithful elderly ladies in a cold church lounge on a Wednesday evening – powerful though this is, it's the exciting, town/citywide, inter-denominational, multi-generational kind of prayer that is fuelling these transformational festivals. Leaders and members alike putting aside doctrinal differences and joining hearts and minds in unison around the Great Commission, embracing like a long lost friend the core truth that the Gospel is most effective when seen as well as heard. Prayer and unity – these are the essential elements. God loves it when brothers and sisters in Christ harmonise in philosophy and practice and seek His face for their land.

Notes

1. See www.soulsurvivor.com/uk/about/history for brief history of Message 2000.
2. www.message.org.uk/
3. www.soulsurvivor.com
4. "Make A Difference" was the name of a long-running Police-led project aimed at getting young people to do something worthwhile in their community during school holidays. It had only limited success over previous years and the Message 2000 vision complemented it perfectly, which was a great encouragement to Bob.
5. See *City-Changing Prayer*, pp. 149ff.
6. www.festivalofhope08.com
7. www.hope.ac.uk/thebighope
8. See www.citylinks.org.uk
9. www.joshuatrust.co.uk
10. www.beaonline.org.uk/
11. www.offthefence.org.uk
12. www.lightproject.org.uk
13. www.ne1online.org
14. www.impactpreston.com
15. www.summermadness.co.uk/festival

The Festival Model: International

Beachfest – Santa Cruz

As I mentioned in the last chapter, a few years ago I was privileged to be part of a team invited to visit California (someone has to make these sacrifices for the kingdom!) as a guest of the Luis Palau Evangelistic Association.[1] They were keen for us to take a look at their new outreach idea which was a huge departure from their traditional large-scale theatre style presentations of the Gospel.

It was about as different as it gets! Firstly, it was not set in a football stadium as most of Luis's missions had been for decades, it was totally outdoors, with the Pacific Ocean lapping at our heels. Secondly, it would last a whole weekend and thirdly it was so much more than a platform-led event. There were a number of different stages from which different nationally known Christian bands would perform throughout the day, punctuating their performances with short, punchy Gospel challenges. I had heard of dc Talk but began to feel my age when the other names were listed and I realised I was well and truly out of touch with the Christian music scene: Kirk Franklin, Jaci Velasquez, plus ONE, Crystal Lewis, Skillet, Plankeye, Pillar, Fasedown and Bob Carlisle – all very big names indeed, not only among Christians, but in the secular charts as well. There was a huge skate park, featuring exhibition displays from world class professional skaters. A children's area provided all kinds of fun activities for kids of every age. And the whole thing had been organised and sponsored by over 200 local churches so that no visitor would have to pay an admission fee.

As we arrived a couple of days before the event, teams were gathering to pray with a high expectation of what God would do. I felt quite challenged by my total lack of faith. Would they attract anything like the huge crowds they hoped and prayed for?

The Palau team, well used to huge attendances at their festivals, was expecting a crowd. Nothing could have prepared me for the first day of the festival when in excess of 110,000 people showed up. My eyes were opened and something inside my heart changed. We returned home with the faith to believe that this sort of model could indeed work in the UK – and the rest is history.

The Palau festival model has been a huge influence on the UK festivals and we are so grateful to them. Surprisingly though, we have discovered that the UK festival model also had an influence on them. This chapter shows how festivals around the world are reaching multiple thousands of people for Christ each year, in word and deed.

The Heartland Story: Luis Palau

A more recent example of a Palau festival took place in Omaha, Nebraska on 16th July, 2007, and here is an extract from their report:

> "The largest faith celebration ever presented in Nebraska wrapped up Sunday night, July 15th, at the Qwest Center Omaha grounds after two days of the Luis Palau Heartland Festival.[2] Event organisers set the weekend attendance at close to one hundred and five thousand people.

The Luis Palau Association has been presenting evangelistic outreach events in the U.S. and around the world for over forty years. At the invitation of over one hundred churches and key leaders of the business and civic community, they began plans to bring a Luis Palau Festival to Omaha.

By 1996 Palau had led evangelistic 'crusades' in fifteen US cities, but felt it may be time for a change: 'We were on the verge of saying, "Okay, maybe somehow God doesn't want us in America." The crowds were okay, but we weren't getting through,' Palau says. 'We began to realize that the classic campaign model – uniformed choir, the suits on the platform, the old hymns – wasn't the way to go for us. We want to attract the un-churched; we want them to encounter God. We want to bring them all to Christ and to understand and to connect. We also want to unite and energize the Church community wherever we go.'

At the suggestion of his sons, Palau moved to the current method of festival evangelism in 1999. Since then, more than six and a half million people have heard the Good News at a Palau festival.

'A nation will not be moved by timid methods,' says Palau. 'Today's young people understand music and technology, but few have an understanding of what a life walked in faith can produce. They don't know the person of Jesus Christ – that He is alive, that He is divine, and that He wants every one of us to know Him personally.'

Before, during and after:

Even in the week leading up to the festival, hundreds of documented decisions were made for Christ! Luis shared the Good News at various events including luncheons, church services and press conferences. 'I am a broken-hearted woman,' said one after a luncheon with Luis. 'Two divorces. A sixteen-year-old granddaughter killed five weeks ago in a car accident. Life is hard, lonely and sad. But I commit my life to the Lord.' Amazing! That's what the Heartland Festival is all about! It's about single moms like Beth, who came to the festival with a friend and recommitted her life to Jesus Christ. It's about teenagers like Danae and Anne, who were brought to the festival by their parents, heard the Good News, and received Jesus Christ into their hearts for the first time. It's about children like eight year old Melissa, who committed her life to the Lord, filled out a decision card, and prayed with a counsellor. She scribbled on the back of her card (in clear eight-year-old handwriting), 'I am very happy to have Jesus in my life!'

The Festival aimed to bring believers together, to encourage them through prayer, and to show the Heartland what Christians are for, not what they are against. To create networks among churches, parishes and believers who will continue those relationships long after the Festival has come and gone. To present the Gospel in a welcoming festival environment of music, action sports, family fun and more. Palau explains, 'We want to bring believers together across denominations through volunteering, counselling and serving. We want the region to see the hands and feet of Jesus through acts of community service.'

A team of world evangelists joined Luis Palau, along with over two hundred and seventy five churches, dozens of local and national businesses, and more than six thousand volunteers to bring the faith festival to the Heartland. All the team meetings began and ended with prayer, along with a number of 'prayer warriors' around the world praying for the Palau Festival and ministry.

As result of ongoing prayer support, many prayers were answered: the festival was endorsed by the regional Archdiocese and participated by twelve Catholic parishes; it had support from some of the Heartland's key leaders; over six thousand volunteers came forward; fifteen tons of food were collected for the hungry; all financial responsibilities were covered, and [understandably important to the Brits reading] the festival experienced unseasonably pleasant weather!

Many well known entertainers in country, pop, gospel and contemporary Christian music performed, including TobyMac, Jeremy Camp, Kirk Franklin, Salvador, Mandisa, Building 429, KJ52, Matt Maher, Heartland and El Trio de Hoy.

Good news for the poor:

A food drive collected close to thirty thousand pounds of food that will be distributed to fourteen regional food banks. A Habitat for Humanity home was built in partnership with the Festival, and a Sudanese family who had lost everything was presented with the keys during ceremonies on Sunday night.

At the close of Festival week, more than five and a half thousand souls had made a documented first-time commitment or rededication to Jesus Christ!

The Heartland Festival has left more than just memories. The Youth Network formed to assist the 'Livin It' skateboard team continues to flourish. Pre-existing events such as the 'Step Out' compassion project doubled its volunteers in 2007 to over six thousand and boosted its church participation from three to twenty-two.

Palau comments, 'The cooperation and unity of the churches, city officials, business and civic leaders was spectacular. We're confident that, with God's grace, the spirit of unity and purpose that was borne out of the festival will continue in the Heartland for years to come.' ''

Lindz West

Lindz (formerly of The Tribe and now LZ7[3] fame) became involved in the Palau festivals following Festival:Manchester where the Palau Association worked with the Festival: Manchester team. The Palau team invited Lindz to join them at events from the American Heartland (Omaha, Nebraska) to the Middle East (Cairo, Egypt). Kevin Palau (Executive Vice President of The Luis Palau Association) says of Lindz, "His boundless energy, creative talent and intense love for His Lord enable him to connect with young people and touch their hearts. Lindz is a gifted, one-of-a-kind servant of God who lives his life at full-speed with his focus always on Christ." Lindz has been the host for the Palau festivals in the states and worldwide for a year now. He has hosted five festivals with three next year already booked. Lindz MCs the stage event together between acts and Luis preaching.

Lindz comments, "Festival:Manchester had a profound effect on the Palau festivals, hugely encouraging them to get more involved on the social action front. The Palau Association now engage with local projects and charities from each city they visit, helping financially as well as getting volunteers involved from the partner churches. The UK has definitely had an influential impact on international festivals."

Kevin Palau supports Lindz's comment and believes that Festival:Manchester was a turning point for the Palau team as they worked with The Message Trust and others:

> "... who humbly showed the face of Jesus with their servant hearts and commitment to social action. To this day, the photographs taken at the service projects in some of the bleakest areas of the city of Manchester remind us of the power and potential of our faith. It can be surely said that the 'Summer of Service' which is now a part of our major festivals was born out of the spirit and example of the UK festivals."

Fusion International

Fusion[4] is another model of international festival involving Christian youth and community organisations. It was founded by Mal Garvin and emerged in 1960 as a response to socially-at-risk young people in suburban Sydney, Australia. Today, Fusion has over two hundred and fifty staff and thousands of volunteers in thirty centres around Australia, European bases in the United Kingdom and Germany, and also works in Albania, Canada, Ghana, Greece, India, Indonesia and the Caribbean.

Fusion has been running Open Crowd Festivals for thirty years. The work has been growing to such a degree that now one in five Australians has attended a Fusion festival! During the Sydney Olympics alone, a quarter of a million people attended Fusion's Opening Night and Torch Run Festivals.

They believe that providing an individual with meaning and community enables them to become resilient and better able to cope with the crises that life brings. Their services seek to build community and purpose. 'Fusion Centres' are established in response to research of local need and in Australia this has led Fusion into such things as:

- Drop-in centres and Youth Cafés
- Lunch-time programmes in schools
- Accommodation programmes for youth, families and High School students who cannot stay at home while completing their education
- Craft and social activities for isolated women and parenting programmes for young single mothers
- Mentoring and other special programmes for teenagers who are not fitting into the school system
- Employment training schemes
- Outdoor education programmes
- Community festivals designed to build connection in fragmented towns and suburbs.

The Fusion team are involved in all levels of youth and welfare networks, including peak national and state bodies. Working closely with local authorities and agencies, in several regions they have been invited by local councils to provide the youth services for the region. Marty Woods says:

> "A distinctive of an Open Crowd Festival is that, at its heart is a small group of friends who love God, love each other and their community and have done the work to know how to create the space and atmosphere where everyone (regardless of age, gender, creed, ethnicity or class) feels warmly invited to and can find themselves resonating with the values of God's kingdom. The Festivals are fun and spontaneous, smiles are shared and people like who they become as they join with others. It is a place where children are the stars, the centre of the community, where we create a safe place and we see together what the kingdom looks like.
>
> We believe and have shown that that if you run Open Crowd festivals three days in a row, for at least three hours each, three times a year for three years, it is possible to birth a national movement founded on kingdom values. A good example of this is in Albania where Fusion International has been working with local teams producing tangible transformation in their communities.
>
> It was only seventeen years ago that Albania was a Communist country where the government prided itself on being the first truly atheistic nation in the world. Recently, a team from Fusion International returned for the third year to the centre of Korce, a city in the south of the country. Our first three festivals were in the main streets of central Korce. The Mayor heard we were returning and arranged to have the main street closed to give us the prime location in the city. From the first night there was a local team of ninety working together and another one hundred and thirty people (mostly young) volunteered to help and began identifying themselves as Fusion. Each took their role seriously and cared for the children, a significant change from our first visit. After three nights of festivals in Korce we had many young people join the

team. Interestingly, this time it was not the parents, or the older teens that joined us, it was the ten to fourteen year olds. These young Albanians were drawn to finding their place and warmly rose to the roles, so much so that many of them came to help run our next set of festivals in a nearby town, Maliq, a twenty minute drive away.

In Maliq, a city closer to the capital Tirana, we had the opportunity, because of the success of Festivals in Korce, to have the Mayor also offer to open the centre of the city for Fusion. Maliq, a community of ten thousand people, is renowned for being one of the roughest places in the region. Stories are told of missionary groups being spat at and having rocks and tomatoes thrown at them. We discovered these challenges on the first night. As we moved into the second hour of the festival, the crowd became unsettled when loud fire crackers were thrown into the crowd, young kids were frightened and then the power went off making it impossible to run the activities. We were able to address the crowd and let them know we would be returning the following night and the Police would be present. We asked people to help us identify those who were responsible for the crackers. As we were packing up, we met some of those who had thrown the crackers, engaged with them and invited them to join us on the team the following night, helping keep the peace. Some in fact came up to us and handed over their crackers.

The next two nights were settled and a transformation took place. It was miraculous that within the Albanian culture hundreds and hundreds of Albanian young people were co-operating. No-one had seen this before. The Mayor said that we had brought something to the city that they had never been able to do. We had won the streets.

The local team grew from six to thirty and on the last night one hundred and thirty young people wanted to be part of Kids Clubs, junior and senior Daytrips and to help run festivals in the future. Reflecting on the impact of festivals in these two cities, there is a verse that seems like the story of Albania:

> 'They will rebuild the ancient ruins
>   and restore the places long devastated;
> they will renew the ruined cities
>   that have been devastated for generations . . .
> For as the soil makes the sprout come up
>   and a garden causes seeds to grow,
> so the Sovereign LORD will make righteousness and praise
>   spring up before all nations.'
>
> (Isaiah 61:4, 11)"

Four years ago now Fusion Youth and Community began running Open Crowd Festivals in the UK. They are continuing to run them across the UK and have big dreams for hundreds of Open Crowd Festivals on the opening night of the Olympics in 2012.

Gemeinsam für Berlin (Together for Berlin)

In December 2001, the interdenominational non-profit association Gemeinsam für Berlin (Together for Berlin)[5] was founded. The intention was not to establish a new organisation, but to provide a network for relationships built on mutual trust that will include existing networks and serve local congregations. The steering committee and the board of the association are made up of representatives from the Lutheran church (Landeskirche), Free Churches, the Evangelical Alliance, the charismatic pastors' meetings, international churches, ministry organisations and para-church organisations.

The Together for Berlin initiative holds the constant involvement of prayer at the top of its agenda:

"Concerted prayer is, and should remain, the first priority of both the leadership and the intercessors from the various churches. In prayer we look for God's will for the Body of Christ and our city and for a unified vision in how to put His will into practice. We believe that God's love has life-changing power and that through prayer, He changes people and circumstances."

As a result, a leaders' prayer breakfast was established to offer a broad basis for people to meet, build trust, share ideas and pray.

Since Together for Berlin was started, deliberate prayer has increased vastly! It now has:

- Major prayer events (three to four times a year a citywide prayer service takes place)
- One-time events like "50 days of prayer for Berlin" (2003) which inspired "40 days of prayer for Germany"
- Prayer info (the monthly Berlin prayer letter in German and English) is a helpful tool for many individuals and churches who are praying for Berlin
- Specific prayer outreaches/actions for events, for example when there is a danger of rioting or other negative influences for the city.

A leader of the initiative commented:

"In 1998/9 there was an initiative called 'Prayer lift' in remembrance of the airlift 1948/1949 that provided food and materials for the city and kept the people alive in a time of distress. Dozens of prayer teams from all over the world (Africa, Asia, America and Europe) came to pray with us and for us. We see the changes that we experience now also as a result of their prayers."

As a result of Together for Berlin they have seen several inspiring initiatives come together through prayer, commitment and a unified desire to see things change for the better: partnerships between various churches and ministries have been developed, forums have been established to help individuals and churches work together and connect in prayer, a Christian Volunteer Agency was started in 2005 to help churches and individuals serving the needy in the city and Together for Berlin is working in partnership with other city networks.

Change on May Day

Leaders have reported:

> "For about two decades April 30 and May 1 were days of rioting and destruction. Anarchists used the traditional 'Labour day' to demonstrate for their goals in their way, with millions of Euros worth of damage and hundreds of people injured in the process. Since we started praying (at first in church buildings, later with mobile prayer teams as well as teams collecting rubbish and bottles on the streets) riots have decreased in strength year by year. In 2006 a newspaper headline read: 'The most peaceful May day in almost two decades.' Violence has not yet come down to zero, but to 0.5%. Christians were welcomed to play a part in the May Day celebrations and a public open air service is held every year since 2004."

In 2007 Together for Berlin are connected with people from about one hundred and twenty churches in the city. About fifteen local churches and three mission organisations are supporting the project spiritually and financially. They are partnering with the Evangelical Alliance in the city and nationwide and with the Ecumenical Council of Berlin. In

February 2008, Together For Berlin will host a National festival-style conference called "Transform". I have been invited to speak at the conference and will be taking a team with me from the UK.

Calling All Nations: Worship in Berlin

In June 1997, Noel Richards and friends saw almost forty-five thousand people gather at Wembley stadium to turn the temple of English football into a temple of worship for one glorious day. Shortly before the Wembley Stadium Event in 1997 some friends of Noel Richards were asking God, "Where do we go from here?" They felt, along with a lot of other people, that Wembley was the beginning of a journey and not the end.

Berlin caught the imagination of Noel and his team. A few days later Noel was reading a book called *The Football Grounds of Europe*. It described a bell that was used to signal the start of the Olympic Games held there in 1936.

> "On the south concourse stands the stadium's original bell. This 16.5 ton monster was cast in Bochum in 1935 and transported in triumphal procession to Berlin, where atop the bell tower it signalled the start and finish of the Games. When unearthed from the bombed ruins of the Maifeld (adjacent to the stadium) – as late as 1956 – the bell was found, fittingly, to have a deep crack through the swastika on its rim, where is etched the motto, *I summon the youth of the world*."

When Noel read these words, he thought, wouldn't it be wonderful to gather the youth of the world and the young at heart for a completely different purpose – to worship Jesus the Champion of the world, to pray for revival, to call the people to get right with God and to receive a fresh commission to take the Gospel to every nation!

During 2003 a date was formally agreed with the stadium for June 2005. Noel released an album in 2004 entitled *Road to Berlin*. During difficulties with the contract, the German advisers felt that the only way the event could happen was if they took on the responsibility for the whole event and worked in support of Noel and his team from the UK. Thus a wonderful partnership between the UK and Germany was formalised. Gerhard Kehl was appointed to run the event and secure contracts with the stadium.

Eventually, the stadium offered a date, 15th July, 2006, just six days after the World Cup Final. Contracts were signed and in April 2005, the planning began in earnest. The fruit of this partnership between the two nations was the Calling All Nations[6] event at the Olympic Stadium.

This was a day when dreams were born, fresh vision was born, hope was renewed and a generation made a promise to serve the King and His kingdom. Almost twenty-five thousand people joined together from over forty countries to praise God in unity.

Global networking

As I hear about these international festivals, which are literally reaching many thousands of people for Christ, I am particularly encouraged by the way in which we are inspiring one another across nations. Good ideas and transformation stories travel quickly and the nations where there is already a growing prayer network and co-operation between churches are those who can make the most of the opportunities a festival brings. Above all, these festivals are increasingly sharing the Good News of the Gospel of Jesus Christ in both word *and deed*. If there is any truth in the saying "actions speak louder than words" then this has to be a God idea.

Notes

1. www.palau.org
2. www.heartlandfestival.com
3. www.LZ7.co.uk
4. www.fusion.org.au
5. www.gfberlin.de/english
6. www.callingallnations.com

Praying and Policing in Partnership

Real people

When I first began to think about praying for our Police force in Greater Manchester, back in 1997, I thought of the Police as a kind of impersonal body; a faceless organisation that existed to protect our way of life. Since then I have become close friends with a number of police officers and have gained a clear understanding of the job they do and the pressures they experience. I've also become aware of the person behind the badge and have been embarrassed at how easily I had lost touch with the simple fact that every police officer is also a normal human being with the same needs, challenges, hopes and fears as the rest of us.

The personal stories in this chapter are reminders of how significant these social servants are and how grateful we should be for their sacrificial commitment (in some cases, like that of Stephen Oake, the sacrifice they give is the ultimate one of laying down their life). Similarly, the feedback from the many different groups working in partnership with the Police on crime reduction projects should not only encourage us to give thanks to the Lord for what He is doing around our nation, but also inspire us to do likewise in our own immediate communities.

Neil Wain's story

Stockport's Chief Superintendent, Neil Wain, has been a passionate supporter of ROC from the very beginning. His first taste of praying and policing in partnership came a few years ago on his first shift as a newly-promoted Superintendent, a Friday night stint that started as the sun was disappearing and the pubs were filling up. He wanted to make a good impression on his new colleagues and so he gave them all a strong pep talk and they took to the streets ready for action. "I was going to show them what proper policing was all about," he explains. "I was hoping we would break some arrest record and fill the cells with law-breakers." As the night wore on, however, it became clear that the only record likely to be broken would be the one they least expected on what is normally one of the busiest nights of the week. Call after call came through to the control room, all reporting the same uncanny news: no crime at all. It wasn't until dawn was breaking that Neil remembered something quite important about the previous day – he'd been prayed for on the Friday morning by a group of Christians who had specifically asked the Lord to give him a trouble-free start in his new job! He didn't know whether to laugh or cry, but he did know something: specific prayers are the most effective sort, especially in terms of crime reduction.

As Chairman of the Greater Manchester Police Christian Police Association[1] (one of the most active branches in the country with a growing membership), Neil is a champion of many faith-based initiatives such as the Eden Project, Street Pastors and the Adopt a Cop scheme. Neil and his colleagues are prayed for by many people through Adopt a Cop. He meets with church members every Friday morning to pray. But he hasn't always lived like this.

In his early twenties, after two years at Art College, one year at university, and hours of time spent with his band

"Abdominal Pain", Neil enrolled at Police training college in 1981. On finishing, Neil quickly became a "copper's copper", one of the "old school", whose attitude to offenders quickly developed into an anger towards them.

He also grew ruthlessly ambitious and decided he would rise through the ranks of the force, which he says was driven by his "love of money". He was also known to be bad tempered and have a foul mouth. Things were about to change, when Neil met Jane, a Christian police officer. As Neil began to like Jane more and more, he began attending church just for the chance to see her! The sermons and the singing went over his head, but he was happy to attend and it made him feel morally good. Neil eventually married Jane, though his church attendance subsequently dropped off.

In the late 1990s, without any reason in particular, Neil felt prompted to return to church once again. Neil began to feel uncomfortable as almost every word spoken during the sermons seemed to be speaking about him! One evening, just before Christmas, he found a Bible and began to read the Gospel of Mark. "There were no blinding lights, no angelic singing," he recalls, "but something inside me stirred and I fell to my knees and asked God's forgiveness. I instantly knew for certain that Jesus Christ had died on the cross for my sins and I committed my life to Him without reservation or condition."

The next time he went on duty it was a new Neil Wain. Colleagues and staff knew almost immediately that "something was different about the Sergeant". Gone was the bad language and selfish ambition.

Neil's faith deepened quickly as he devoured his Bible and other Christian books. He couldn't stop talking about Jesus to everyone, colleagues or criminals! During this time Neil's atheist parents listened to the Gospel and committed their lives to Christ.

During the 1990s Neil rose through the ranks of the Police force and promotions happened in quick succession. In 2001,

Neil won a scholarship and was seconded for six months to the John Jay College of Criminal Justice in New York, to teach British policing skills to the NYPD and FBI. Not long before taking up the position, Neil read a book called *Cop for Christ* that tells the testimony of a hard-hearted New York police officer, Mike Dzanza, and his coming to faith as he lay seriously injured and dying on the streets of New York. The two Christian cops made contact via email and a meeting was set up for Neil to meet Detective Carlos Aviles, the NYPD president of New York's Police officers for Christ. The morning of 11th September Neil was due to attend a meeting at 1 Police Plaza, the NYPD's HQ, near to the financial district of Manhattan with a clear view of the World Trade Centre.

As he prepared that morning for the meeting, the first of two hijacked planes slammed into one of the towers followed minutes later by a second. Neil could only run backwards and forward between his window and the television as the events rapidly unfolded. Like so many around the world who witnessed the attacks, he found it hard to fully comprehend what he was witnessing. Later on that day he received a phone call from Carlos Aviles who simply said, "We need your help down here, brother." It was in the early hours of the morning that the two met, standing on the mountain of rubble and twisted metal that became Ground Zero.

One of Neil's own officers had lost a lifelong friend in the attack and wanted to visit New York for himself. Ian arrived in New York in time for a memorial service for his best friend, whose body was never recovered. Neil and the others could see the depth of grief in the younger officer's heart. They prayed for him. As he tried to come to terms with his loss, Ian heard and saw the Gospel in action. When Neil returned to Manchester in January, Ian came to see him. Speaking excitedly he told Neil that he could not forget the conversations he heard in New York and needed to know more about Jesus. Neil invited Ian to an Alpha Course. Before the course had finished Ian committed his life to Christ, the grief and pain replaced by peace and joy. Today, Ian is a powerful witness and testifies to the redeeming, healing power of God's salvation through faith in Jesus.

The threat of terrorism came back to the UK and again profoundly impacted Neil's life when fellow officer and Christian brother DC Steve Oake was stabbed to death during an anti-terrorist raid in January 2003 in Manchester. Neil was appointed by his superiors to oversee Steve's funeral at Manchester Cathedral which was attended by thousands who lined the streets to pay their respects, along with the Prime Minister and his wife.

It was Steve's death that has prompted Neil to make a desperate plea for prayer and support for police officers as they face the ever-increasing threat of terrorism and gang-related killings. Neil wholeheartedly believes the prayer and positive action of local churches, as well as individual Christians, has helped reduce crime in Stockport. He has testified this before Members of Parliament who have applauded and supported his beliefs. Home Office statistics show a reduction in crime rates in Stockport has occurred. As Neil learned a while ago, with God all things are possible, including crime-free Friday nights!

Kirstie, Steve and Andrew: Lancashire

In 2007 I was delighted to be invited to speak to church and community leaders from the Fylde Coast. There was a real interest in finding out more about how they could build on their experience with working with the Police. Inspector Kirstie Banks-Lyon from Lancashire Police attended the meeting and was encouraged to see the enthusiasm of the church leaders about working with the Police. She brought along a colleague, Steve Cowles, who works as a Chaplain with Lancashire Police. He said that Police stations across Lancashire would be keen to link up with local churches and wanted to know how quickly that could be arranged! We are finding quite frequently now that the Police are initiating relationships with the Church rather than the other way around.

Here is Kirstie's story:

> "I became a Christian at the age of fourteen through the work of Scripture Union, Scotland,[2] in my secondary school, and around that time I decided that I wanted to join the Police. I always thought that I would join Strathclyde Police, but God had other ideas, so at the age of 20 I was accepted into Lancashire Police and moved 180 miles from my family, church and friends. I was confident at that time that it was God's plan for my life and moved to the area excited about my future. The reality of shifts and loneliness soon hit home and along with the premature death of my mother from cancer I gradually stopped going to church and my faith dwindled. However, God still had His hand on my life and He kept nudging me to return to Him.
>
> About seven years ago a friend asked me, once again, to come along to her church. As usual I said I would, but had no intention of going. However, on the Sunday morning I felt that it was time to stop running and attended her church, where I have been ever since. Mind you, she did give my daughter a part in a nativity play so I had to come back the next week and bring my husband and eldest daughter with me! My husband and children have now all become Christians.
>
> In June 2005 I was promoted to the rank of Inspector. On the day I was promoted, a Christian colleague gave me a circulation list of ten people that he sent the Redeeming Our Communities monthly national prayer bulletin[3] to and said that as he was retiring could I take it on! Little did I know at that time what that bulletin would lead to! I now circulate electronically the ROC Bulletin to fifty people and a branch of the Christian Police Association has been reformed.

Eighteen months ago I moved into the area of Neighbourhood Policing and Licensing and came into contact with a Christian group called Fylde T3.[4] At my first meeting I took copies of the ROC DVD with me, as I was excited about the Church in the Blackpool area linking in with the Police. In the last few months the links have grown and I have spoken at a prayer concert about the need for churches to come together and pray for the Police. I am excited about the future, for Hope08[5] and for the churches linking in with police officers and praying for them for the work that they do. It is a tough job, but I am glad that God called me to do it, and despite my shortcomings, He can and is using me for His glory."

Colours nailed to the mast

Also from Lancashire, Andrew Pratt, Chief Superintendent of the National Community Tension Team, speaks about what it is like to be a Christian in the Police force and just how valuable support from other Christians can be:

"I joined the Police in 1982 motivated to try and make a difference after having seen the urban riots in 1981 in Manchester and Liverpool. I was a Christian when I joined and I remember my recruit interview which included this question: what are the three most important things in your life? I decided to nail my colours to the mast. I replied, my Christian faith, my family (married with a one daughter) and thirdly my work. I was not sure how this would be taken by the interview panel. They obviously weighed this up along with everything else I had said and took me on. I wasn't sure if they were going to reject me outright for being a religious nut.

I have been open about my faith over the past twenty-five years and have experienced times when I thought I had no friends and times when I have seen the grace of God at work in people and circumstances.

The Police force is a pretty secular organisation and people of any faith find it hard to fit in. I have tried to be true to the three priorities in my interview and the big drinking culture of the 1980s meant that I was a bit of an outsider. Until recently, I have found it hard to find a local church that understands or tries to support their police officers and this has been an issue for me over my service. The Church and society in general are full of negative stereotypes about the Police which means that the occupation is at best seen as low status and at worst a corrupt occupation and certainly not a calling from God.

I have taken great encouragement from the faith and witness of fellow police officers and have tried to be a support for them in return. The last few years in Lancashire have seen a growth in prayer amongst police officers and staff. I have found this to be where real growth has taken place. The times of prayer with colleagues have been times of deep moments and I have truly hungered and thirsted after those times.

I really have seen prayer transform communities when the local Christians have got together with the Police and put prayer and practical effort into helping.

My role at the moment is right at the heart of the Police response to counter terrorism. I see this as a spiritual battle and encourage all Christians to pray against the powers of evil. To pray for their communities that God would bridge the hatred that exists in them. To pray for wisdom for the detectives. To pray for the Muslims who feel victimised by the press and that Christians could be Good Samaritans to them and show them God's love. To pray that we would be able to stop any terrorist attacks and arrest the offenders."

Roger Bartlett: Barnstaple

In June 2007, I was representing the ROC initiative on a speaking tour in the South West. On 24th June over three hundred and fifty people gathered for a citywide prayer meeting at The Grosvenor Centre in Barnstaple. The meeting was attended by local police officer Roger Bartlett and by Tony Melville, Deputy Chief of Police for Devon and Cornwall (the largest Police district in the UK covering Devon, Cornwall and the Isles of Scilly). Pastor Dave Samms from Living Wells Church had organised the meetings and plans to continue drawing the churches in Barnstaple together. Tony Melville told us that crime had fallen by 6% since the churches had been gathering to pray and violent crime had fallen by one third.

Roger comments on how churches began to work with the Police in Barnstaple:

> "The Lord laid on the hearts of a few Christian officers that we should form an active branch of the CPA (Christian Police Association) in order to support Christian officers, share God's love with colleagues, proclaim the Gospel with everyone we come into contact with and to link in with churches in order to encourage them to pray and respond to the issues of crime and disorder within their communities. We all recognise that God had called us to the Police service as our mission field and that this provided unique opportunities to build God's kingdom on Earth as it is in Heaven. They have recently been using 'Care for the Family' resources to help their non-Christian colleagues in their family lives. More recently they have been encouraging churches to respond to the needs of their communities by promoting united prayer, linking with local Police, considering street pastors, supporting ex-offenders and running courses such as 'Drug proof your kids'."

Roger now attends regular prayer events in Barnstaple to raise issues of local concern. On one occasion there had been an extensive series of dwelling burglaries that was believed to be down to one individual. The group prayed specifically that

God would trip up the offender in order that he would be caught. Within three days of these prayers, the offender was arrested, having been seen by a passer-by leaving premises that the witness knew to be empty. The witness saw the offender get on the bus, followed it, ringing the Police who stopped the bus and found the offender in possession of items of jewellery from the premises. The offender was jailed and the burglaries stopped.

The same group prayed in the lead up to Halloween that God would prevent any anti-social behaviour which in the previous year had left the Police unable to cope and many people feeling fearful and distressed. That year the Police in Barnstaple did not receive a single call to any incidents of damage or disorder which was unprecedented! There are many other examples, including the seizure of a large amount of drugs the same week that the group had prayed for God to impact upon the supply of drugs in the town. Amazing!

The church in Barnstaple has a drop-in centre which has recently helped two men, both heroin addicts, involved with dealing and prolific offenders (138 and 178 convictions, each containing multiple offences). Through their interaction with the drop-in centre and the church, both men have now been clean for three and four years respectively, and have begun operating a Sunday soup run in the town. Their lives have been radically transformed by the power of God! One of these two is now a manager of the Christian recovery project he was once a resident at and the other is working with the Drug Action Team as a mobile needle exchange worker. Both are now married, one with two children.

Mike Parsons from the Freedom Centre[6] in Barnstaple says, "This has attracted a lot of attention with the Police and they have had them speak at Christian Police events as well as on radio interviews about church and Police partnership working. Even non-Christian policemen are acknowledging the role the Christian community has to play in reducing crime."

Anthony Delaney: Surrey

A former police officer, Anthony Delaney[7] leads a church in Surrey. He joined Manchester's Police Cadets in 1981 and left the Police having been a PC for almost ten years, in 1992. He was living a hard drinking and womanising life until, from no church background, he had a dramatic conversion experience through what he describes as "a full-on vision of Jesus" while driving to work. It was not quite the road to Damascus, but the road through Gorton. He reckons that he owes his personal faith in Jesus to the fervent prayers of a group of Christians who used to pray every day for the Police station he worked at in Cheetham Hill (North Manchester).

The last year has seen many new opportunities for ministry with the Police. Anthony has been invited to be Chaplain to the Police in Surrey and joined their IAG diversity group to represent Christians as one of many "minority groups" to give opinions on policing strategies.

Hundreds of officers in Surrey and the Met gathered in Dorking Hall to discuss how best to engage with their communities, where Anthony was invited to speak about ROC as Area Co-ordinator. At this meeting he talked about the parable of the Good Samaritan, emphasising that Jesus spoke about who was a neighbour: the one who crossed the road and got involved, linking this in with neighbourhood policing. Since then, many more opportunities have opened up. During Hope08 several interdenominational prayer meetings will take place and Anthony has been invited to speak at various policing forums and "diversity groups". He invited every police officer in Surrey to this year's carol concert where the speaker was J. John and there was input from the local CPA representative.

Assistant Chief Constable of Surrey, Lynne Owens, herself a Christian, prayed at the ROC Surrey launch and then challenged churches to be more accessible and to work in partnership with the Police for the benefit of all, praying for their local neighbourhood teams and getting "clued up" about crime. Lynne said, "As Surrey Police seeks to embed our Safer Neighbourhood teams in the heart of every locality in Surrey, it is really exciting that churches are hearing and responding to the call to redeem communities. One of the challenges of policing is that to be truly effective we need to engage with all the communities we serve and work with them, and partners, to respond to issues as they are raised. Clearly we cannot achieve this mission alone and members of all faith groups are important and accessible members of local areas. I think that a willingness to work together to identify problems but equally, and perhaps more importantly, to jointly work on sometimes very practical solutions, could make a real difference to the County in which I both live and work. In my view this project could see tangible success in making a significant impact on people's lives if Christians really are committed to sacrifice their time, buildings and skills for the benefit of their local communities."

It definitely seems like the spiritual landscape is changing throughout our nation and it is likely that this is just the beginning.

Neighbourhood policing[8]

One really exciting door that is opening up in the UK at the moment is the new Neighbourhood Policing strategy which will be nationwide by March 2008. For those of us old enough to remember the local beat bobby, this is a simple concept to grasp: local police officers who take time to get to know the community and its people, increasing the emphasis on crime prevention through befriending people and developing trust. This will present loads of new opportunities for churches and Police to work together, starting with the easy task of getting to know the individual inside the uniform and beginning to pray for them as ordinary people.

I was visiting a Salvation Army church in my home town recently and I spotted a poster on the wall with photographs of the local Neighbourhood Policing Team. This church had already begun to take seriously the idea of praying for their local police officers and, although just finding out names and putting pictures on a wall may only be a small first step to take, it could represent a very important beginning to a whole new way of redeeming a community.

The Neighbourhood Policing scheme was introduced after a government white paper, *Building Community, Beating Crime*, recommended that police teams be tailored to the "local needs of local communities". Different areas are to have dedicated teams to provide familiar faces of reassurance to the community. The scheme hopes to enable the Police to work in partnership with voluntary groups, churches, local government, criminal justice agencies and others.

Martin Bagshaw, the programme manager for the National Policing Improvement Agency in Neighbourhood Policing, tells us how vital he feels neighbourhood policing is and the importance of partnering with community and religious groups:

"I have seen first hand how Christian groups and organisations can make a significant and telling contribution when working alongside and supporting local neighbourhood teams to improve the quality of life in local communities. The enthusiasm, dedication and commitment of the church community is heart warming. This was nowhere more evident than when I had the privilege to attend the Redeeming Our Communities launch event in Birmingham in 2006. I was overpowered by the sheer enthusiasm and warmth of those present, their absolute desire to help improve the life of local communities and their willingness to take personal responsibility for doing so.

Like most other police officers I joined the Police force to protect and serve the people who lived in the communities I was responsible for. This desire to serve has been with me throughout my career. Effective policing, however, is sometimes a complex process and one of the frustrations I have wrestled with, as many officers have, is trying to meet all the demands and targets placed on us, in many cases conflicting with each other. One of the main difficulties has always been trying to provide people with reassurance, confidence and safety in the places they live and work whilst at the same time meeting all the other responsibilities placed on us with the resources available.

The Service has now learnt the importance of providing a visible local presence in communities and in addressing the concerns that communities raise with us, especially in relation to anti-social behaviour and disorder. The neighbourhood policing approach taken by forces in England and Wales is now making a real difference in improving confidence in the Police. However, to be really effective it requires the positive and active involvement and ownership of communities, public safety agencies and voluntary organisations. One of the cornerstones of effective neighbourhood policing is that most local problems cannot be solved in the long term without communities taking responsibility and ownership of them.

Neighbourhood policing works. This is due to the commitment and dedication of local neighbourhood policing teams and their partners. However, the demands placed on the Police Service continue and delivering neighbourhood policing alongside these other demands will continue to be a significant challenge. The commitment and participation of voluntary organisations such as Redeeming Our Communities is therefore crucial its continued success. Without such involvement the opportunity now open to us to make long lasting and permanent improvements to people's lives may be missed."

Christian Police Association (CPA)

The Christian Police Association[9] has been around for almost 125 years, founded by Catherine Gurney in 1883. From its inception its *raison d'être* has been to care for the Police both physically and prayerfully. Apart from caring for both Christian and non-Christian officers when tragedy strikes, or fingers of blame are pointed, the CPA also seeks sensitively to spread the Christian message, forge links with churches and provide Christian resources like its *Cops and Robbers* magazine. In many ways the CPA has paved the way for the remarkable stories we're hearing these days of churches beginning to link up in partnership with police forces all around the country. Don Axcell, CPA's Executive Director says:

> "In some areas where churches have been specific in their prayers, there have been annual crime reductions of 30–40%. It can also lead to tangible service in the community. One church that was linked with their local police force and actively supporting them in prayer had a call for assistance one Sunday morning. An elderly person had collapsed and the Police had needed to break into the property to assist and get the lady to hospital. A company to secure the premises was not available for some time, so members of the church with appropriate skills came to the rescue after their morning service was over. This was to the amazement of the Police and to the eternal thanks of the occupier."

Many parts of the country have set up initiatives to pray for the Police, like the one in Lincoln. The Lincolnshire Christian Police Association have launched a "Prayer Watch" where Police and Christian groups get emails alerting them to crimes in their area, allowing congregations to focus their prayers on specific incidents such as burglaries and violent attacks.

Lincolnshire road fatalities were increasing and despite the best intentions of the Lincolnshire Road Safety Partnership these annual figures were showing no signs of decrease. Lincolnshire was at the top of the league for road deaths per capita of population. Brian Keel, Pastor of New Life Christian Fellowship, writes, "A small group of concerned people met because we sensed that, as believers, we could not just accept the present situation, but that we were being 'encouraged by the Holy Spirit' to do something. 'Lincs to Prayer' started in 2002 and has been building up good relationships with the local Police force and seeing results."

Inspector Andy McManus of Lincolnshire Christian Police Association admitted he was expecting a sceptical response: "I know that praying can make a difference in my work, but it's all a question of faith," he said. He claimed winter casualty rates on the roads have been cut since the Bishop of Lincoln started blessing the council's fleet of gritting lorries: "We pray over the gritters in the winter and the casualty reduction rate has plummeted, it really has."

The Lincolnshire Police published these figures:

Year	Seriously injured	Fatalities
2002	739	104
2003	627	93
2004	517	74
2005	438	69
2006	330	64

Adopt-A-Cop

The CPA encourages churches up and down the country to "adopt a cop".[10] Adopt-A-Cop started ten years ago and has been working successfully all over the country. It's a brilliant way of showing our Police, individually and as a group, that we care about them and that we support their pursuit of crime reduction, peace and a strong community.

Churches commit themselves to adopting, in prayer and friendship, all who work in their local Police Station, both police officers and civilians. A coordinator at the Police Station supplies information for prayer on a regular basis, such as areas of potential disorder, as well as personal needs such as joyful occasions, weddings, birthdays. Churches also adopt individual police officers or larger groups praying by name or corporately.

"Get to know your police officers and pray for them," Don Axcell said at the national launch of ROC in Birmingham in May 2006. Don has recently been developing more resources to inform us about how to pray (see Appendix 2, "CPA: Pray4Your Police Suggestions").

IMPACT

In August 2002 Mick Connolly and wife Lyn were struck by tragedy when their son Paul was murdered. Mick leads Wavertree Christian Fellowship in Liverpool, and shortly after this horrific event, he and Lyn made the incredible decision to forgive Paul's attackers and seek reconciliation and healing.

Just six weeks after the murder, Mick and Lyn attended the launch of IMPACT: In Merseyside Police And Churches Together".[11] IMPACT was initiated by Dave Riley and Tom McLelland, two police officers. It links the Police in Merseyside with one hundred and eighty churches, organisations and individuals. An appeal was made at the launch for a prayer coordinator and Lyn agreed to take on the role.

For the first three years Lyn met with a "link" person from the Police who would share concerns and specific prayer requests which Lyn would then mail out to churches in the Liverpool south area asking them to pray.

Currently Lyn and Mick have almost two hundred

churches, organisations and individuals on their prayer mailing list for Police and crime issues. Doors have opened for them in many other ways to share the message of the Gospel with the lost, including Lyn now visiting Walton Prison to share with the men there.

As a result, the Police in Merseyside are feeling the support and encouragement of the local church. Rowland Moore, from Merseyside Police Community Relations Department and Superintendent comments, "IMPACT is unique, and as a partnership provides the greatest support to the Police service of any collaboration I know."

Street Angels

The Chief Constable of West Yorkshire Police, Sir Norman Bettison, explains why 8,000 volunteers each year are joining Halifax's "Street Angels"[12] to demonstrate God's kingdom as reality on the street:

> "Street Angels is an initiative of Churches Together in Halifax[13] and Halifax YMCA[14] working on Friday and Saturday between 9 p.m. and 3 a.m. Based at the Fair-trade café on Crossley Street, volunteers wander the town and ensure the safety and protection of those who become vulnerable in any way. Halifax has seen a 42% reduction in violent crime over 2006. Street Angels launched in Halifax in November 2005 as a response by the Church in the town to the problems on Friday and Saturday nights. Street Angels have assisted 2,000 people. Following the success in Halifax, churches and Police have formed partnerships launching Street Angels in Wakefield, Huddersfield, Manchester and Harrogate, with Bradford, Pontefract and Wetherby starting soon."

Local Police cite it as the main reason for a 40% drop in crime in the town centre. Street Angels received the Duke of York's community initiative awards in October 2007, presented by HRH Prince Andrew at an Awards event in Conisburgh, Doncaster.

Street Pastors

Street Pastors is an initiative originating in Kingston, Jamaica, where churches banded together to take their faith onto the streets. Street Pastors arrived in the UK in 2003, spearheaded by Les Isaac[15] in London. 2007 has seen a sharp rise in the number of towns and cities starting up the initiative, with Aberdeen, Chelmsford, Swindon, Norwich, Romford, Portsmouth and Colchester joining Leeds, Manchester, London, Birmingham and Weston-super-Mare. Many more cities are planning to pioneer or expand existing programmes.

Street Pastors patrol the streets from 10 p.m. until 4 a.m., usually on a Friday or Saturday night. All street pastors receive training in counselling, drug awareness, sociology, knowing their community, role and responsibility and street safety. It's not about preaching the Gospel, but about listening, caring, helping and working in an unconditional way. It's helping people know the local church is there for them in a practical way.

They talk to everyone from dealers to those who just hang around. Street Pastors work alongside Police, but not with the Police. It is important that the community they are serving know that they will not be passing on information to the Police. Areas where street pastors have been introduced have seen dramatic decreases in crime rates and as a result the Police are increasingly supportive of the initiative.

The rapid spread of Street Pastors across our country presents a real opportunity for the Church of Jesus Christ to become relevant to a community that has no experience at all of church.

Developing partnerships with the Police

The key to building a successful long term relationship with the Police is to build up trust and confidence. I have heard messages of caution from a good number of senior officers aimed at deterring enthusiastic but poorly prepared Christians from rushing into their local Station brandishing a Bible. It's so important to follow these tried and approved steps:

- Link up with other churches or organisations in the neighbourhood to avoid duplication
- Nominate one person to serve as a contact and establish a point of contact within the neighbourhood police scheme and know their role. Neighbourhood police teams have police officers, police community support officers and volunteers
- Be appropriate and sensitive with your use of language. Don't use Christian jargon or preach judgment, instead say "thank you", let them know they are appreciated. Work with them, volunteer on crime reduction strategies, but above all deliver what you say you will deliver and have prayer as your foundation.[16]

Here are a couple of prayers, written specifically with the Police in mind:

> Blessed are you, Lord, God of mercy, who through your Son gave us a marvellous example of charity and the great commandment of love for one another. Send down your blessings on these your servants, who so generously devote themselves to helping others. Grant them courage when they are afraid, wisdom when they must make quick decisions, strength when they are weary, and compassion in all their work. When the alarm sounds and they are called to aid both friend and stranger, let them faithfully serve you in their neighbourhood. We ask this through Christ our Lord. Amen.[17]

Almighty God, who has committed into the hands of men the good ordering of Thy world, we pray for those in Thy Name who are responsible for law and order, especially the men and women of the Police. Give them confidence in their high calling as Thy ministers for good. Grant them the ready support of all Thy people in keeping the peace, and do Thou guard and guide them in all their daily duties, through Him who not be ministered unto, but to minister, even Thy Son, Jesus Christ our Lord. Amen.[18]

Notes

1. www.gmcpa.org
2. www.suscotland.org.uk
3. www.redeemingourcommunities.org.uk
4. www.ft3.co.uk
5. www.hope08.com
6. www.freedomtrust.org.uk
7. Author of *The Don't Have To Do List*, published by New Wine Press, and the forthcoming, *How To Have The BEST Marriage*. Anthony leads a church in Surrey. (www.l1fe.org)
8. www.neighbourhoodpolicing.co.uk. The key person in pioneering this initiative is Chief Constable Matt Baggott of Leicestershire Police.
9. www.cpauk.net
10. www.adoptacop.com
11. www.impactmerseyside.co.uk
12. www.streetangels.org.uk
13. www.churchestogetherhalifax.org.uk
14. www.ymca.org.uk
15. www.streetpastors.org.uk. Les is the author or the book *Relevant Church, A God-Given Goal: An Inspirational Journey into Ministry and Church Life* (Ascension Trust, 2004).
16. For further information, useful resources include the City Links "Step By Step Guide" and their "Guide for Police Officers" at www.citylinks.org.uk, and the CPA "Pray 4 Your Police" suggestions at www.CPAuk.net
17. Diana Macalintal MA, Director of Worship for Diocese of San Jose and University Lecturer for University of Minnesota, Institute in Pastoral Ministries.
18. Prayer for the Police, by Canon Eric Saxon.

Appendix 1

Redeeming Our Communities: Developing Partnerships with the Police

How can we develop partnerships?

Once you have begun to pray, you can begin to tackle the issue of how we can develop partnerships with criminal justice agencies, particularly the Police.

The aim of developing partnerships is to join the earthly with the spiritual to see transformation in communities. We can use the earthly intelligence provided by data and analysis from our local neighbourhood policing teams to inform our prayers in the spiritual dimension. The priority of ROC is not to convert as many police officers as possible, the priority is to see communities transformed. Police officers coming to Christ may be a by-product, but it should not be the aim.

What is Neighbourhood Policing?

There is a new policing strategy being rolled out across the UK called Neighbourhood Policing. This is a practical way of delivering change in our Police forces across the UK.

There are three themes to the Neighbourhood Policing approach:

1. To create permanent and dedicated teams that will have specific responsibility for each defined neighbourhood and will become familiar faces to those who live and work in that area.

2. These teams will use the National Intelligence Model to direct their activities – focusing on those problems that the public have told Police matter most to them.
3. Neighbourhood teams will work closely, and take joint action, with local authorities, voluntary groups, businesses, criminal justice agencies and other partners to tackle these issues.

In practice this will mean that individuals and communities will benefit from:

- *More visible and accessible policing* – regular contact with the same local officers.
- *Having a better say* – with more effective ways of identifying and responding to what local people see as priorities.
- *Holding people to account* – the public will know exactly who is responsible for reducing crime in their area.

The UK has been split into divisions and neighbourhoods in which policing teams will be located, the aim being that they will systematically engage with the needs of the community.

For example:
Greater Manchester Police is divided into twelve divisions. Each division is separated into Neighbourhood Policing Teams, comprising a dedicated team of sergeants, constables and Police Community Support Officers, and headed up by an inspector. The Neighbourhood Policing Teams have been set up to respond to the needs of local communities and not only deal with crime related issues, but also ensure that local people are happy with the quality of life in their area.

Within ROC we can tap into this resource to make us more effective.

There are some things that we would like to encourage you to do:

What can we do?

Simply say "thank you" to our police officers
Police officers need to be encouraged and affirmed. They have an extremely challenging job and work every day with broken and chaotic people. We can be the one voice of encouragement they hear. We can offer them simple acts of kindness to demonstrate that we appreciate who they are and what they do.

Pray for the police officers in your area specifically by name
You can use the "Adopt-A-Cop" scheme run by the Christian Police Association. Go to www.cpauk.net/adopt for more details. Or find out the name of your neighbourhood policing officer and commit to praying for them.

Volunteer
The Police are always looking for people to join neighbourhood watch schemes, become a Special Constable, or assist on crime reduction schemes. Find out if there is anything you are able to do and do it.

Assist the Police in the work they are doing
We can report crimes and provide information. If your local Police authority has this system (RSS feeds), we can put information on our church websites and pray for current needs.

Approach your neighbourhood policing teams to find out the needs of your communities.
This information can inform your prayers. Find out what areas of crime and disorder the Police are aiming to tackle in your area and support them in prayer. Make an initial point of

contact to the Inspector heading up your local neighbourhood team.

Remember, we must do this appropriately:

- Be aware of the language you use and how you communicate.
- We need to keep in mind that we are trying to build a long-term relationship and need to build up trust and confidence with police officers.
- Confidentiality is important. We will hear of general needs, but we may become privy to specific information that must be regarded as confidential amongst our prayer groups.
- We need to be clear about our expectations of each other.

Appendix 2

Christian Police Association:
Pray 4 Your Police Suggestions

- Contact your local Police Station and find out the names of the Neighbourhood Policing Team officers for your area. Pray for them by name.
- Regularly obtain a copy of your local newspaper and look for reports where officers have been injured on duty and pray for them.
- Using your local newspaper, list reports of local crime and pray that the Police will be successful in apprehending the perpetrators.
- Listen to local radio and television news and take note of any items involving the Police that need praying about.
- Log on to your local Police website and navigate to the news/appeals page where you can find local items to fuel your prayers.
- Pray for God's protection on your local area that you will have peace and an absence of crime.
- Find out the name of the senior police officer in charge of your area and pray for him/her and all the staff (both police and support staff) who work under their command.
- Whenever you see a Police vehicle, whether or not they are on an emergency call, pray for the crew. If it is responding to an emergency call, pray for the safety of the officers and for the situation to which they are going.

Appendix 3

Redeeming Our Communities:
Guidance for Police Officers

- ROC aims to encourage churches to support their local police officers with prayer and active participation in making their communities safer places to live.
- Churches represent all sectors of society and provide a good source of information about local concerns and problems in the community which can help form the way we police our neighbourhoods.
- Engaging with your churches will provide an opportunity for your policing priorities to be promoted to a willing audience which will extend to their family and friends. Police updates can be provided in church services or via newsletters etc.
- Working with churches will increase community contacts and may encourage recruitment for neighbourhood watch schemes, the Special Constabulary, PCSOs and the regular Police service.
- Christians believe that God answers prayer. Your local churches will be keen to pray for their Neighbourhood Policing Teams and for crime reduction in their area. Sharing general crime data (e.g. vehicle crime rising on neighbourhood 3) will encourage churches to pray specifically for hotspots and could generate information to assist the Police.
- The church's single point of contact (SPOC) should be identified and updated regularly on local crime trends. Promoting your force website and Neighbourhood

Policing Team website with churches will assist this flow of information/communication.

- Inviting your local churches to consultative groups and public meetings will enhance diversity and develop healthier partnership working.
- "Voluntary and Community Engagement" usually features as a core priority within your local authority community safety plan. Working within the ROC model will evidence this work stream and empower your churches to assist in tackling local issues, demonstrating meaningful working partnership.
- ROC is not about converting people to Christianity, but encouraging people to be helpful active citizens, contributing to a better quality of life for all the community.
- And finally ... churches/parishioners provide great tea stops!

A Captive Audience

"I was in prison and you came to visit me."

(Matthew 25:36)

If we want to see crime reduced in our communities we're going to have to do something to address the issues that affect the people who commit crimes – 80,000 of whom are behind bars at any given time.

There is a huge polarization between the backgrounds of criminals and non-offenders. Statistics show that the majority of offenders have suffered social, educational and material deprivation.[1] A 2002 Social Exclusion Unit report shows most prisoners come from socially excluded backgrounds. They are thirteen times more likely to have been in care and fourteen times more likely to be unemployed when compared with non-offenders. 52% of male prisoners and 71% of female prisoners have no educational qualifications.[2] On top of this, it's clear that their experience in prison, while serving as a punishment and, hopefully, a deterrent, actually further reinforces a number of existing problems.

It's exciting to hear reports from all around the UK of how God is touching so many lives in prison, especially amongst young people who still have a good chance of breaking out of the cycle of re-offending that seems inevitable to so many.

God seems to be opening many avenues up for Christians to not only visit people in prison, but also to share the Gospel and work with them in a number of different ways. For example, in November 2006 a week-long mission in a prison near Uttoxeter, Staffordshire, saw 120 prisoners give their lives to Christ. Ray Duckworth, Deputy Director of the prison, testifies to miraculous healings, changes in personality, and a real peace among inmates who made a commitment. It is estimated that 20% of the prison population are now Christians!

This chapter outlines some examples of how Christian groups and individuals are reaching out to this neglected group of people, getting right to the heart of the issue and pushing the boundaries of community restoration.

Reflex[3]

Youth For Christ developed a project called Reflex to engage with young offenders. They provide them means of learning new skills and opportunities to overcome the barriers they face. "Locdown" explores themes like addiction, peer pressure, discrimination and trust through music which can eventually be released through Locdown Records. "Inside Out" is a dynamic urban theatre project combining contemporary film, music and theatre to challenge perceptions, raise self-awareness and explore different points of view.

"Mettle" is a discipleship programme for Christians, those who attend chapel and people who have been on an Alpha course. It is designed to encourage the growth of Christlike qualities and help them to make informed choices about their futures. When a young person joins Mettle they are given the opportunity to sign up to a resettlement programme. Upon release they are linked to local churches who, through a small group of volunteers, care for and support the young person. There are currently 700 of these courses running in the UK.

After assessment, a young person is paired with a mentor from the church who will visit them while in custody and be a positive role model. Letters are written via a Reflex post office allowing addresses to remain confidential. When a young person leaves custody they face many challenges, both practical and emotional. Reflex works in partnership with statutory and voluntary agencies to provide comprehensive and tailored support. Three volunteers from the church are required: one is a mentor providing care, support and spiritual guidance, another is a practical helper assisting with forms, budgeting, cooking and other needs, the third is a friend, someone to get alongside ex-offenders and introduce into friendship groups. All are trained in child protection and behaviour management.

Mark's story

Mark (not his real name) was in prison, aged eighteen, for unlawful wounding. He had suffered a lot of pain since the death of his mother and this had led to a lifestyle of drugs, alcohol and crime. One night, in a drug-fuelled rage, he seriously assaulted his father. This led to a complete break-down in their relationship and time in jail. During his time in prison, Mark hit rock bottom, even considering suicide. It was at this point that God worked a miracle in his life and he became a Christian. Through prayer, he and his dad were able to face each other once again and be reconciled to one another. Mark apologised to him and through God's grace, his dad has been able to offer forgiveness.

Mark recognised that if the changes taking place were going to last, he wouldn't be able to do it alone. Reflex worked with him whilst he was still in prison, providing some support to him and helping him to make arrangements for his release and to plan his future. Once released, a worker from Reflex met Mark and chatted with him on the phone on a regular basis to provide ongoing support and challenge behaviour. They introduced him to a local church and provided him with a volunteer mentor to offer pastoral, spiritual and practical support. Soon, he will be setting up home on his own for the first time. Reflex will help him to find a tenancy, furnish the property and learn the skills required for independent living. Mark has experienced some real difficulties and challenges since leaving prison, but Reflex has provided support to help him succeed. He has also enjoyed many successes, some small, some great, and Reflex has celebrated with him. He says that it's mainly due to Reflex that he's where he is today.

Since leaving prison Mark has kept away from drugs, alcohol and the acquaintances who shared these things with him. He is studying at university and working part-time. He is living with his father and helping to bring up his first child. He has also been leading some assemblies in his local high school, sharing his story and encouraging others to stay away from drugs. He has also spoken at several churches and events sharing his inspirational story of hope and a life transformed by God.

Reflex has played a major part helping Mark to stay away from crime and in enabling him to play a full and positive role in his local community.

Partners in the Gospel

In the North West of England, YFC works in partnership with The Message to deliver Reflex into a number of Young Offenders' Institutions. The results have been incredible with hundreds of young people regularly connecting with the Gospel through many creative methods.

I recently heard an amazing testimony from a women's prison: Anne (not her real name) was dramatically converted in early 2007. She had been a repeat offender for some years, was addicted to hard drugs and prone to outbursts of violence.

All the inmates (and most of the warders) were afraid of her and treated her with caution, keeping their distance where possible. Through the personal contact of one of the young women on the Reflex team, she gradually began to open up and talk about her life, eventually making a commitment to Christ. The change was immediate and quite remarkable. The new Anne was (and still is) calm and at peace with herself, completely uninterested in drugs, reading the Bible and praying for all her fellow prisoners and guards. She became a one-woman Christian revival ministry, leading women to Jesus on an almost daily basis. Anne was due for release on 27th December, 2007, but her behaviour became so exemplary that the Governor called her into his office and told her she was to be considered for parole, which would mean she could leave a few months early. Her reaction was one of extreme emotion. Although not the one you might have expected, rather than beaming from ear to ear and jumping for joy, she was distraught! The thought of leaving behind her newly converted friends filled her with sadness. "Please, please, let me stay," Anne begged the Governor. "I want to serve my full sentence." Bemused, he agreed and Anne went back to her cell praising God that she would spend Christmas in prison!

There are so many stories to tell from the tremendous work of Reflex in these Young Offenders' Institutions. Lives are being changed completely by the power of God and the service of dedicated missionaries, all of which points in the direction of community transformation. Once these young men and women emerge after their sentences, many of them not only remain "on the straight and narrow" but also become part of the solution to the problems of their own communities by getting involved with a church (Reflex help with this as well) and often becoming volunteers in prison work themselves.

I was going to edit the following testimony to straighten out the grammar and spelling but, in the end, decided it was better to use the original (although I have changed his name).

John's story

"My name is John and my story starts about five years ago in
2002. I was about 15 years old and my mum and dad split up
and me and my mum moved out. This put a lot of pressure on
me because I loved my mum and dad and I was being
pressured over who I wanted to live with. My schooling was
being affected and I started to play truant and hanging around
with an older set of friends who didn't have jobs and made
their money from selling drugs and doing robberies. I quickly
got involved in what my friends was doing and within no time
I was getting a name for myself and was getting arrested
frequently. I was soon a persistent young offender and was in
front of the youth court every week. I was even on first name
terms with the security guards. After a while there was no
other punishments the courts could give me and I finally got
my first custodial sentence at 16, but I wasn't bothered. I had a
lot of friends in jail and I knew I'd be ok, but I was in for a big
shock half way through my sentence.

I got a visit off the chaplaincy telling me my dad was very
poorly and was going to die. This was a big surprise. I'd only
seen him 2 weeks ago on a visit and he was fine. The
chaplaincy went on to say that he'd had a stroke and when
taken to hospital after a few checks they learned he had lung
cancer. I was distraught. My dad was my hero. He couldn't die
whilst I was in here could he. But things just got worse. He
had another stroke and was took back to hospital where he
went into a sort of coma. This is when I first started praying. I
prayed that he'd be ok and that he'd get through this but my
prayers weren't working. He was just getting worse.

After about a week I knew he was suffering and so was my
family and I changed my prayers this time. I prayed that his
suffering would stop and God would just take him. I just didn't
want him to hurt no more. My prayers were answered and that
night there was a phone call to prison off my sister who had

not left his side since he was took to hospital. She told the officers my dad had got really bad and the nurses didn't think he'd make it through the night and asked if I'd be able to say my goodbyes. The officers allowed it and my sister put the bedside phone to my dad's ear and I told him how much I loved him and how proud I was going to make him. He couldn't talk back but when my sister came back on the phone she asked me what I'd said because he'd started smiling and hadn't even made a reaction for a week up until then. It was a very emotional call and even the officers that were in the room was crying. I said my final goodbye and went up to my room and broke down. I didn't sleep a wink that night and wasn't surprised when the chapel came in my room the next morning and told me my dad had passed away through the night.

A few months later I was released and on the right path. I'd got an apprenticeship in engineering working on the trains and metro link and found a nice girlfriend who I am still with by the way. But then a year down the line the unthinkable happened. My mother was diagnosed with breast cancer. I was distraught and for some stupid reason I started to hang around with my old friends, but they was into bigger things now carrying guns, selling hard drugs and committing armed robberies. As quickly as the first time, I got involved in it. Me and my girlfriend started arguing and my family knew I was up to no good. I was always dressed nicely, had expensive jewellery on and had bought myself a ten thousand pound car. I didn't care what my family and my girlfriend was saying. I was enjoying this life, but it didn't last long. We did a gunpoint robbery at a jeweller's and got away with £33,000 worth of jewellery and money. I was caught quickly and put on remand pending trial.

Again I didn't care, I wasn't even thinking about changing my ways. I was kept on remand for 6 months then sentenced to 6 years for the robbery and moved to the jail where I abide now. I was just getting on with my time when an officer came in my class and told me I'd been put forward to do a DJ course run by Reflex. I thought to myself who's put me forward? I've only been here for a couple of weeks. Surely the teachers would put forward someone they know. I now know it was God who put me on this list and this would be the start of my Christian adventure.

That week I started the DJ course and had no idea it was run by Christians. I think I even heard someone saying they were Christian, but I didn't believe it. I thought Christians don't do things like this. They just Bible bash. I had a really good time on the course and near the end found out they were Christians. I was very interested in this new style of Christian and started asking a lot of questions. One of them told me that they was doing a service in the chapel that weekend and that I was more than welcome to come. I went along that Sunday and I loved it. I'd always believed in God but really just didn't understand it. I showed a lot of interest and one of the Reflex team told me about a course they ran called Alpha on a Thursday. I joined that and really enjoyed it. It taught me a lot about Jesus and the Bible and I started spending all my time reading the Bible and praying.

I loved this new meaning in my life and was filled with the Holy Spirit, telling everybody how Jesus had come into my life. I told my mum all about the team and about me becoming a Christian and she was really happy and started crying. She's better now by the way and has beat the cancer and has now got the all clear. When Lucy my girlfriend heard she was happy too but told me that she didn't want to be a Christian because she wanted to be a police woman. Bless her, she thought being a Christian meant you had to do the type of job the Reflex team does. I've explained it to her now and she's all for it.

I still have a lot to learn about Jesus and Christianity but I'm learning it. I still don't know what teacher put my name forward for that DJ course. As far as I'm concerned it was God who did it and it was the best thing that has ever happened to me!''

Cops and Robbers [4]

Paul Senior spent over twenty years in the Metropolitan police. In 2004, as a member of the Christian Police Association, he came across a scheme in Northamptonshire called "From Crimes to Christ" where written testimonies of ex-offenders, now Christian, were put into cells for prisoners to read.

Paul thought this was an excellent idea and proposed something similar, but doing the stories in comic book form as some people have problems with literacy and, for some, English is not their first language. This was a means of bringing hope to young people caught up in crime.

"Everyone has a testimony," Paul says. "Cops, robbers, ex-prisoners and other people. No two are identical, though some have one thing in common: a complete change after encountering Jesus Christ and becoming Christians."

Initially, there were some problems gaining permission to distribute the comic, *Cops and Robbers*. First it was granted, then suddenly revoked. Paul explains, "On New Year's Eve 2005 God spoke to me about the coming year being a year of promise for 'you and your children'." On 2nd January 2006 the *Daily Mail* published an article stating the comic had been censored. The BBC picked up on the *Cops and Robbers* story and details were told of how one person's life had been changed by the power of God! Eventually, after much prayer, distribution of the comic was finally approved.

Ten thousand copies of the first edition were published and given away. The third edition, "Hope, inspirational true stories" has just been published. The comics are sold over the Internet and provided free to all prison chaplains in the country through Holy Trinity Brompton. To increase circulation they have tried to make them more politically acceptable and suitable for schools without compromising the Christian message.

Devon and Cornwall Youth Offending Team have seen a number of young people come to faith after reading *Cops and Robbers*. The comics have spread abroad with reports from Canada that, "the prisoners enjoy them because they are hardcore, telling them as it is." God has provided finance, opportunities for distribution and even an artist, Al Gray.

Workout

Steve Rawlins received his first prison sentence in 1986 for robbery and his last in 1996, when he was sentenced to thirteen years for drug trafficking. He served seven years and was released in 2003. It was while serving his sentence that he became a Christian. His new found faith inspired him to study for a degree, train as a Samaritan to support suicidal prisoners, and work alongside prison chaplains to devise programmes to help inmates deal with various issues. Steve, aged forty-one, serves as manager of a project called The Workout Project in Elephant and Castle, South London. The project launched in May 2005 is a charity helping unemployed ex-offenders find work. Many of its clients are referred by statutory and voluntary agencies and staff members make contact with inmates prior to their release, offering them help in getting work and accommodation. Mentors are often put forward by Street Pastors projects and churches. The mentors support former inmates as they progress to community living.

Upon their release, the ex-inmate is met by a member of the Workout team as soon as possible, given a place on a life skills training induction course and given a voluntary work place-ment. Workout clients also meet with a job coach who helps them compile a CV, develop interview techniques and find a job.

One success is Robert. He was in prison for burglary. He went through the Workout programme for two months, after which he got a job as a trainee drug counsellor and has now been in a job for over twelve months. "Workout is brilliant," he says. "They believed in me and helped me gain the skills and confidence I didn't have. Now I just want to help others to find the way of life that I have found."

Offenders Anonymous [5]

One interesting new angle on the subject of persistent offending has led to the formation of a new organisation, one that follows the tried and tested approach of the mutual support, group therapy programme, used so effectively by Alcoholics Anonymous.[6] The theory is that some persistent offenders are actually addicted to crime and they need to be helped to kick the habit. One member of OA, Steve, says, "Burglary was the crime that gave me the biggest rush. The power of knowing that this house, this flat I was in belonged to me. It was mine, because I was in there and I was in control."

Top criminal psychologist John E. Hodge says for some offenders, crime may be a physical and psychological addiction, little different from being hooked on heroin or alcohol. Hodge, who was Head of Psychology at Rampton, says: "It is well known that a relatively small proportion of criminals account for a very large proportion of crime. For some of those people, their criminal behaviour itself may have become addictive." He argues that the recognised characteristics of addiction, such as the need to escalate the behaviour to produce the same high, cravings, and unpleasant withdrawal symptoms, do not only apply to substances such as alcohol or heroin. They can also apply to behaviour such as gambling, jogging or crime.

Offenders Anonymous aims to reach out to people like Steve and help them kick the crime habit for good. Founder member Rob, forty-eight, firmly believes that a proportion of persistent offenders are compulsively drawn to repeat their behaviour: "This is a new way of looking at persistent or prolific offenders. It will be a real switch (for officers) to see them as addicted criminals."

Offenders Anonymous is pioneering the methods first adopted by Alcoholics Anonymous in the 1930s. Addicts work through a 12-step programme: the first step is to admit your addiction and clearly identify yourself as an addict. Self-help groups hold regular meetings that offer essential support through what can be a crushing struggle to beat addiction. The organisation is still in its embryonic stage with just two branches in Hoddeston and Twickenham, and a sister organisation, Gang Members Anonymous,[7] founded by a group of prisoners in Mule Creek Prison, California. The organisation hopes to expand across the country and into prisons where essential work could be done to help prevent prisoners re-offending on their release.

Rob describes the desperate point he'd reached with shoplifting, burglary, alcohol and drugs. Taking the plunge into a 12-step programme was the start of a genuine recovery from his addictions. "It gets you to look in depth at yourself. To have a very clear and honest look at what drives you, at what your behaviour, your history has been. That was very painful, but the support of the group got me through it. It provides a safe place to open up and be honest. The 12-step programme was full of realisation after realisation. It was gobsmacking stuff."

Fellow OA member John, fifty-eight, is an ex-heroin addict and dealer. He says the first crucial step to recovery is: "Admit you have got a problem and your life is unmanageable. The next, and the critical bit, is accepting it is impossible to do anything about it on your own." John says he found the group a huge source of strength: "It is an intense process of self-discovery at the beginning, but the 12-step programme does also provide a set of tools for daily life."

Both Rob and John are now crime and drug-free and attend monthly meetings of Offenders Anonymous.

Steve's Story

The life of the criminal addicted to crime is typified in the testimony given by Steve Cattell. Steve grew up in the East end of London in what he describes as an unloving home. Behavioural difficulties led to his expulsion from three schools and aged eight he was sent to a psychologist. Shocked to discover he had been adopted, in the seven days following this disclosure he broke into seven houses on his street. At ten years of age, he was placed in solitary confinement in a secure unit, in a soundproof cell with bars, a concrete bed and a fireproof mattress. Following his release aged thirteen and upon discovering his foster family were paid to look after him, he burgled their house. He hated the world and wanted to commit as much crime as possible to get back at it.

Aged fifteen he was sent to a young offenders' prison, spending much of his time in punishment blocks, fighting with inmates and being beaten and abused by those in charge. Full of hatred and anger he left prison and from eighteen to thirty-two he was locked into a cycle of offending and imprisonment. Opening the door of someone else's property gave him a powerful buzz, like an addict taking cocaine. Rarely sleeping, when he did, he dreamed of burglaries. On the way to prison from court he would look out of the van windows for burglaries to do when the gates opened and on release would do as many as he could. He says, "A criminal psychologist helped me understand that I have an addiction to crime."

He was facing two suspended sentences by two separate judges and would normally have expected six to eight years in prison. Ignoring legal advice, but following the prayerful encouragement of a friend who had recently become a Christian, John made statements admitting the full range of his crimes and telling the judges he wanted to change his life. Miraculously, he escaped two prison sentences and was encouraged to take part in the Offenders Anonymous recovery programme. He says,

"The programme gives me a way to deal with addiction that has been central for as long as I can remember. I know that an important part of the twelve steps programme is to make amends to those people I have hurt (step nine) and when I think of the damage I have caused to so many over the years, I get overwhelmed and shut down, trying to block out memories and feelings. I am now two years crime free, some days are a struggle, but I am blessed with a happy family life."

Barry Woodward: Author of *Once an Addict* [8]

Barry Woodward's start in life was good. He was born in a great home in Salford, Manchester. He struggled at school though and left with no qualifications. It was then he met a group of guys who were taking drugs. They were smoking cannabis, taking amphetamines and using LSD. This seemed like an exciting life to him so Barry started to use drugs too. It wasn't long after this when they all tried heroin. Within six months they were all serious heroin addicts.

Eventually, Barry moved away from his parents in Salford to live in Hulme, near Moss Side, Manchester, and he began to deal drugs in order to feed his own addiction. Meanwhile he started to go out with a woman some ten years his senior. For a time things were going well. He had money, a nice home, respect and all the drugs that he could handle, but then after several arrests he landed himself in Strangeways Prison (now known as Manchester Prison).

Barry ended up in prison on several occasions. One time, after being released from Preston Prison, Barry went on a nine month drugs marathon. Then, right out of the blue, he started to hear evil voices twenty-four hours a day. He was later admitted to Cheadle Royal Psychiatric Unit in Manchester, suffering from Amphetamine psychosis.

After many years Barry eventually moved to Rochdale, and one day he was travelling to the town centre when a guy on the bus started to speak to him. A few days later he met this guy again, coming out of the local hospital grounds. He told him he had come from church. He invited Barry along, but he refused. In the meantime, Barry was settling down in the area and was still suffering from Amphetamine psychosis and went to see a new psychiatrist who continued to prescribe him his medication. He then got speaking to his next door neighbour and asked if she knew were the church was. The woman not only knew where it was, she was a regular church member and offered to take Barry along. Within minutes of them arriving at the church, the man from the bus came in and sat with them and just before the service started he heard, "Hallelujah! Praise the Lord!" He looked behind him and it was his psychiatrist. He began to wonder if these guys had been following him for the last few weeks!

At the end of the meeting the speaker asked people to step forward if they wanted prayer. He couldn't help but get up and go to the front. When the guy started to pray for him he felt like there was fire running through his body, he was hot, he started to sweat, he even started to cry and he was shaking like a leaf. It was a "God Encounter". Since that day Barry hasn't been the same! Within about five weeks he was off all the drugs. It was an absolute miracle!

Within a year of him having this religious experience Barry realised that there was a specific purpose for his life, that God had called him has an evangelist to communicate the message of Christianity. In 1999, while he was at Cliff Bible College, he set up a charity called Proclaim Trust, which now acts as a support base for him and his ministry. Barry is now an associate evangelist with J. John of the Philo Trust.

Prevention is better than cure

They say prevention is better than cure. This is true not only in terms of personal health, but also in a communal sense.

Imagine a community where every member has a sense of pride and belonging, where young people are thriving and active members, using their gifts to contribute to the well-being of society, where the desire to commit crime has been replaced by aspirations of personal development and social welfare. This is the dream we all long for. Christians and Church groups contribute to the making of these healthy communities. But where society and the Church have failed, we have to consider how best to respond. Thank God for those who work with offenders and ex-offenders, inside and outside prison, to enable them to make better lifestyle choices and, in turn, to become part of God's programme of community redemption. These stories of transformed lives prove that change is possible. No one method or programme can make the whole difference, but God is at work in and through a whole variety of excellent agencies and initiatives.

Notes

1. Just one example: literacy. The prison service invites convicted prisoners on reception to volunteer to take a literacy test devised by the Basic Skills Agency equivalent to the reading skills of a nine to ten year old. In 1998 of the 60% of those taking this test, 40% had severe problems. Paul Senior, from the Christian Police Association tells us, "There is a constant stream of people going through the system with very weak literacy. And nearly all of them are barred from well paid and fulfilling employment. Our aim is to get the *Toe by Toe* literacy scheme on every wing and for the probation service to provide continuity in the months after release to those who have not completed their training. Tackling illiteracy will also tackle one of the causes of crime.
2. The Department of Education and Skills in December 2005.
3. www.reflexuk.net
4. www.copsandrobbers.org.uk
5. www.offenders-anonymous.org.uk
6. www.alcoholics-anonymous.org.uk
7. www.angelfire.com/id/CGAnonymous
8. Barry Woodward, *Once An Addict* (Authentic Media, 2007).

CHAPTER 9

Setting Captives Free

What do Pink Floyd, The League of Gentlemen, The Full Monty, the European Capital of Culture and Sybil from Fawlty Towers have in common? . . . Bradford! A small, northern city normally associated with, well, being near Leeds!

Over the last few years, we've heard some depressing stories about race riots and terrorist arrests, but Bradford is also the home of many inspiring Christian initiatives, two of which feature in this chapter as shining examples of redemptive excellence. Both have experienced great growth as the hand of God has honoured them in their commitment to see communities transformed, not only on their own West Yorkshire doorstep, but also in many towns and cities across the country.

Bradford has been bathed in prayer for many years with a strong united prayer movement, Prayer for Bradford, co-ordinated by Howard Astin, the Vicar at St John's, East Bowling. Howard stresses that their priority is to pray for the *people* of Bradford and the surrounding region of West Yorkshire, "that God would bless them, encourage them and challenge them to change where change is necessary. We pray also for kingdom values to prevail such as honesty, integrity, peace and harmony."

He adds, "Additionally we support each other and seek to promote unity between the churches in Bradford. As

Psalm 133 says: 'Where there is unity, there the Lord commands His blessing.' Through this unity we hope to have an increasingly significant Christian voice in the city that both influences and responds to events and issues. We have quarterly prayer meetings with prayer and praise where church ministers and members from across the city can come together to pray and worship together. These are great times. About twenty-five ministers from various churches come together every fortnight for a prayer breakfast. During each breakfast we have a specific area to focus on. This would often involve a Christian to provide knowledge and insight in the area we are praying for that morning.''

This is an increasingly familiar and encouraging situation: Christians putting aside differences to unite in prayer for their city. I'm convinced that it's no coincidence that fruitful ministries always seem to emerge in places where there is this sort of faithful, consistent, united prayer.

Bradford is the birthplace of two of the most excellent examples of community redemption ministries that I have come across anywhere in the UK and I have enjoyed getting to know the key leaders over the last few years: John Kirkby (the founder of Christians Against Poverty)[1] and Mike Royal (National Director of the Lighthouse Group),[2] each of whom has poured their life into realising a God-given vision to help release people from two modern-day forms of social captivity: debt and education crisis.

Both John and Mike heard God speak as each became aware of the seemingly impossible circumstances faced by people in their own locality. They knew that they had to show the love of God in action in order to build bridges of trust between the church and people in need. They also knew that they couldn't achieve very much on their own; they would need to mobilize churches and, somehow, learn to co-operate with secular agencies. Their stories are remarkable testimonies to the grace and power of God and strong indicators that we really are plugging in to His agenda when we organise our energies to pray and act for the poor.

Christians Against Poverty (CAP)

The UK is without doubt one of the world's richest and best resourced countries, the envy of many and the dream destination for hundreds of thousands of immigrants each year. Our schools and colleges are amongst the best in the world and our economy one of the strongest, and yet debt and education continue to present huge challenges to the Government. Britain is top of the European league in terms of personal indebtedness. According to Credit Action the total UK personal debt at the end of June 2007 stood at £1,345bn. This amount is over 10% up on the previous year. Total consumer credit lending to individuals in June 2007 was £214bn. This has increased by 5.2% in the last twelve months. Twenty-one million UK adults have unsecured personal loans averaging £10,200 each (including credit cards, retail hire purchase, overdrafts and personal loans). And most alarmingly of all, Britain's personal debt is increasing by £1 million every four minutes.

Excessive borrowing not only weakens our economy and leaves households exposed to global fluctuations in share values and commodity prices, but also damages individuals and eats away at the fabric of community life. As people succumb to the lure of the "have it all" philosophy that bombards them every day, self-esteem is eroded, dignity is lost and productivity disappears. Marriages are ruined as couples argue over finances and homes are repossessed as their owners drift into a state of emotional paralysis.

Occasionally, these are the very early stage factors in the causes of crime. Desperate, depressed and debt-ridden people can easily turn to unlawful measures to try and make ends meet. Violence is a common outlet for the anger that builds inside a person going through the trauma of financial calamity. For many, especially the poorest in our society, their debts have become the walls and bars of a prison cell. There seems to be no way out, no space, no peace, no freedom.

God cares and calls His people to act against the evil forces that feed on these social circumstances. To share the Gospel in these kinds of contexts, actions must speak before words can be heard.

Christians Against Poverty is one of the organisations seeking to offer advice and support to those most affected by debt. They work across the UK and, at the time of writing, had sixty-six centres. I went to visit the Headquarters of CAP, Jubilee Mill, a few years ago when a friend and colleague from Manchester, Owen Crane, went to work for them. As I walked around the almost completed renovation of an old mill, I was impressed by all the work going on around me. Lots of telephone conversations with clients and different departments dealing with various aspects of CAP's work.

Our whistle stop tour around the offices was suddenly interrupted by the clanging sound of a bell ringing. Owen, my guide, said, "I was hoping this might happen during your visit." Quite intrigued, I noticed everyone was downing tools and leaving their desks. I assumed it must be a fire drill and hoped it wouldn't take long as I wanted to make the most of my visit (although why Owen would want me to experience a fire drill was a strange idea).

I knew I was wrong as everyone began to move, not towards the fire exits but into the centre of the main office where the old-fashioned, wall-mounted bell was situated. Owen explained that whenever one of their clients gives their life to Christ and news of it reaches the office, the bell is rung and the staff all gather to pray and give thanks to God. The bell had been rung two hundred and thirty times between May 2006 and April 2007!

CAP's founder, John Kirkby, became a Christian in 1992. By his own admission, for the next four years he was a bit lukewarm in his faith. However, in early March 1996, there was a sense of change and opportunity. He felt he had a major decision to make. "Either I continued to do it my way and really push for more 'success' or I put myself properly in God's hands to see where He would take me."[3] The department he was responsible for at work was due to see a downturn in profit because of market changes. Consequently, on 9th March 1996, he phoned his boss telling him that he should close the department because of those market changes. As a result, John was made redundant. He was left thinking about what he could do next and how God could use the gifts he had and the experiences he was going through.

He thought through some crazy ideas about what to do with his time and talents, but then a friend simply asked him, "What could you do on your own, now, without any money or anyone to help you start?" John says, "I went straight to my computer. I can't remember even praying. I just typed 'debt counseling'. That was it! I knew this was it. I could start now and get stuck in. I had found something I was qualified and able to do."

John then spent time seeking God's heart for the poor. He studied Scriptures about the poor and our responsibilities to them. He discovered overwhelming evidence throughout the Bible, not only of God's direct heart for the poor, but His heart for justice, fairness and equality throughout society. Two key scriptures stood out and they have subsequently formed the basis for CAP:

> *"Speak up for those who cannot speak for themselves,*
> *   for the rights of all who are destitute.*
> *Speak up and judge fairly;*
> *   defend the rights of the poor and needy."*

(Proverbs 31:8–9)

and

> "The Spirit of the Lord is on me,
>   because He has anointed me
>   to preach good news to the poor.
> He has sent me to proclaim freedom for the prisoners
>   and recovery of sight for the blind,
> to release the oppressed,
>   to proclaim the year of the Lord's favour."

(Luke 4:18–19)

John's own experience of debt had opened his eyes to the misery it inflicts on others. He got into debt after his first marriage failed during a time when all his businesses collapsed. He'd ended up living in a bed-sit with a friend. He literally had nothing. "I was a completely broken man, living in a shell, shattered and breaking up. I remember one time having my kids stay overnight in my bed-sit. We went to the supermarket and I had to put items back at the checkout because I could not pay for them. The word 'destitute' is often over used but that's what I'd become: utterly devoid of any spirit, hurting, lonely and afraid. I now know that God used this and other desperate experiences in my life for good. It was through these traumatic times that a greater sense of His love, forgiveness and heart for me became more and more real. I also began to have an ever-increasing compassion for others who were in need."

As John started visiting people on the local Bradford estates his eyes were opened further as he saw the devastating impact of debt. He knew he could not give this up. "The next three months, up to Christmas, were to fill me with compassion time and time again. I saw things that really opened my eyes: families with hungry children, people in trauma having no hope, broken marriages, and the sheer havoc and distress financial difficulties bring about in people's lives. Their strife had a profound effect on me. They were what inspired me to drive forward and see more people helped. It was strange that right from the first few weeks I knew I was born for this work and the thought of giving up never entered my mind."

Out of this grew CAP, starting with John working from home and then with a small staff of three by the end of 1997. In 1998 they embarked on their first partnership with the local church, Kings Church in Aldershot, and they started their first centre which is still active today. John realised that partnering with the local church was the way to grow. He says, "At this time I knew so little about what I was about to do, but somehow just felt that this was the only way to allow rapid expansion of our work over the coming years." They grew from five centres in 1998 to forty-eight centres in 2006. CAP currently has sixty-six centres in the UK.

God has honoured and blessed CAP and they have grown at a phenomenal rate over the last ten years beginning with a budget of £10,000 which is now nearly £3 million.

CAP aims to show God's love in action by providing sustainable poverty relief through debt counselling, advice and practical help. Their core values are:

- Godly finances – giving godly wisdom to release people from poverty
- Empowering people to manage their finances with greater wisdom and understanding through education and ongoing support
- Teaching people to keep their lives free from the love of money and to be content with what they have (Hebrews 13:5)
- Faith – knowing that God will provide
  - Being sure and certain that God will provide everything we need: strength, motivation and resources to accomplish our vision

- Justice – standing up for the poor and disempowered
  - Bringing justice to those in poverty and debt who do not have the power or influence to change things by themselves. Being fair to both client and creditor
- Local church – partnering with local churches
  - Partnering with local churches so they can effectively help people out of debt and poverty in their communities and so clients can experience the love of God through His family, the Church
- Love and compassion – expressing God's love in practical ways
  - Showing God's love and compassion to those in financial difficulties through a practical service which will see them lifted out of debt and into a whole new life and destiny
- Salvation – seeing people come into a saving relationship with Jesus
  - Bringing an understanding of God's love to people so they have an opportunity to believe and come into an eternal saving relationship with Jesus Christ

John has hundreds of good news stories to tell about people who have found not only a financial lifeline through the ministry of CAP, but who have also come to know and experience the love of God personally as well.

Pete and Nicole's story

Pete's story is just one inspiring example of CAP's effectiveness:

"I wanted to tell you our story because without people like you things would have been very different for me and my family. The Centre had only been open three months when I phoned and I can't imagine where I'd be now if CAP hadn't

been there. We wouldn't have a house, I'd still be failing my
family and I'd be absolutely desperate.

In April '95 my left foot was amputated following an
accident at work. A few years later I took out a loan, but
following a review my Disability Living Allowance was
stopped and I was stuck with a debt I couldn't pay. I set up
my own business as a mechanic, but a year down the line I
suffered a mild stroke that left me unable to work. Nicole was
being exploited by an employer paying less than the minimum
wage. It got to the point where we couldn't afford the shopping
so we'd miss paying a bill so that we could afford to live. We
used to go without the gas so that we could afford the electric,
but that meant warming up kettles of water to bath the kids.
We couldn't afford anything.

Then the difficulties started with our marriage. I was
constantly worrying about the long hours Nicole was working, but she would say that it needed to be done to pay the bills
and put food on the table. It felt like she had all the pressure on
her and I felt a bit useless because I had not long since had my
stroke. I was struggling even to look after the children while
Nicole was out trying to earn enough money to live. We were
just biting each other's heads off all the time. Debt also had an
effect on the children. We were very agitated and tired and we
seemed to shout at them for every little thing. I felt like I'd let
the kids down because I couldn't provide for them.

We stopped opening the letters because we knew what
they all said. I felt better ignoring the situation because it
wasn't getting any better when I was trying to deal with it. We
were just getting further and further into debt. The last letter
that came through the door was a repossession order two
weeks before Christmas. It got to the point that we thought if
they take the house, they'll have taken everything, so we'll
have nothing else to lose. We just felt that life wasn't worth
living any more.

Before phoning CAP we tried a couple of solicitors. One

told us they were sorry but we'd gone too far down the line and the house was as good as gone. That was the same day as we saw the advert for CAP in the paper. We weren't going to bother, but then we thought, it's our last hope, it's got to be worth a try – so I rang.

Dave Tudor (Fleetwood Centre Manager) had to tell us that he didn't know if we could save the house or not, but he was willing to try. At least someone was here to help us. We had to look at council housing as an option and all that was on offer was a one-bedroom flat with no cooking facilities. We had an emergency court hearing the next day, one hour before we were due to be evicted, and fortunately Dave got the case adjourned. It meant that we had a house over Christmas and that was a success in itself.

After Dave's first visit, he kept us in the know as much as he could. Some days he would even ring us to see how we were and it was nice to be treated as an individual and not just another customer. The second time we went to court, it was my little daughter's birthday. We were singing happy birthday to her, trying to keep things normal for the kids, but we knew that an hour later we'd be stood in court and could face losing the house. We couldn't buy her anything for her birthday, but all we hoped for was that she'd have a house to come home to.

The day I found out we could keep the house was amazing. It was like heaven, like having a fresh start. Dave sorted out a budget and we actually had a set amount to live off for shopping which was great. After about 4 or 5 weeks, we could see that the bills were being paid and we started to see the benefits. We could buy the kids the odd little thing at a weekend and we could actually buy a week's shopping and not just have to buy a loaf of bread. We knew it was going to work.

The future looks fantastic now. We can see a life ahead of us, a life for the children. We started going to church through CAP because Dave used to pray with us before going to court and I thought, 'Oh well, it's working, so what's there to lose really?' We had already seen the benefits of praying and believing, so we started on an Alpha Course that Dave invited us to. I became a Christian on the 18th January and after a few sessions Nicole asked God into her life too.

Being a Christian is the best move I've ever made. I thought that believing in God in my head was enough. He's in our lives in a big way now. I realised that Jesus had been with us all the way through. He had been to court with us and had helped us out. He works closely with us and I thank Him for coming into our lives the way He has done and for helping us through. I am soon going to be training to be part of Dave's Support Team. I want to be able to help anyone who's going through what we've been through."

Janet and Eric's story

"When I left work to have my youngest child, things were tight, but we thought we could manage. Then, six months later my husband lost his job and he found it really hard to get a new job because of his age. We got really behind with our bills. I managed to ward off being evicted, but only by borrowing £900 from my ex-father-in-law. I also got a small loan just to put food on the table for my 5 children. But I knew I couldn't repay them and that it was all going to happen again.

I used to go days without any food, just telling the kids I had already eaten. I breastfed my baby until he was 2 because I knew he wouldn't get the vitamins he needed if I didn't. Our marriage hit rock bottom. We couldn't look each other in the eye or even be in the same room. I couldn't tell him that I'd borrowed money, the court letters, the mortgage and the rest – it would have finished him off. We walked past each other in the home and couldn't even give each other eye contact. My husband slept on the sofa for a month, we couldn't even touch each other. He said he was going to leave because he just couldn't cope anymore.

One day I went to the doctor's because I needed something to get me up in a morning. I needed to take care of the children and I was not functioning properly. I walked into the surgery and picked up an 'Are you in debt?' leaflet, got some pills to see me through, went home and made the call.

When I spoke to Bernie (CAP Selby) I felt like she was my best friend. She listened to me when I needed it most. She visited us the next day and we handed over all our paperwork. She asked if she could pray for us and from that moment it felt as though God was on our side.

Bernie came back a week later and told us what to pay when – it was brilliant. We were given a realistic amount to pay off our debts and still put food on the table. To put a small amount away for savings as well was unreal. Bernie asked if we wanted to go on a short break that CAP organised for some clients. The atmosphere was fantastic, relaxing, happy and fulfilling. We wanted to keep this feeling forever and knew it was because God was there. The talks were very good and made us think. I gave my life to God almost straight away and Eric followed a few days later.

We now attend King's Church in Selby, we've been on an Alpha course, and we're looking forward to getting baptised. We've also been on a marriage course and our relationship grows stronger by the day. Our children are happier because we're happier as parents. We want to do all we can to help CAP so we're both now volunteers visiting other families who are in the same position as we were."

The work of Christians Against Poverty is inspirational and life-transforming – not only helping to ease people out of their debt-captivity, but also leading many to spiritual wholeness as well. What began in Bradford has now spread to sixty-six centres throughout the UK. John's story shows what God can do through a person willing to step out and engage with the real needs of people in the community. As John often says, "If God can do it through me, you also qualify."

The Lighthouse Group

Just as the UK is, at one and the same time, one of the world's wealthiest countries and one of the most debt-ridden, it also enjoys one of the best education systems in the world and yet many thousands of young people reach adulthood with no qualifications at all because they couldn't or wouldn't fit in to that system.

Education crisis is another trap that mainly affects people in the poorest areas of our society. The schools are there, usually well-funded and often staffed by excellent and highly motivated teachers (many of whom are Christians called to socially challenged areas by God Himself), but the problem is that many of the young people don't fit in to the system. Sometimes this is because they lack the basics in their upbringing. For others it's the result of immaturity and a series of wrong choices. In every case there is a downward spiral that gets harder to correct. This is the issue addressed by The Lighthouse Group (TLG), another Bradford-based ministry which is now expanding across the UK.

TLG's National Director, Mike Royal, was brought up in the leafy suburbs of Surrey. Born of Jamaican parentage, Mike was aware from an early age that the lifestyle he enjoyed was not typical of that experienced by many black people who had migrated to Britain in the 1950s and 1960s. His parents had become Christians in the early 1960s. Having exchanged the dance hall for the church hall, Mike was raised in a small Pentecostal church along with his two sisters.

Being the son of a head teacher, education was an important part of home life. He was often set homework by his father, who took the time to explain how to do things.

However, his early school experience was rather different. He remarks, "At school I was rarely pushed or encouraged to excel and little effort was made to find out what would really engage me, hence my early schooling reports where pretty average for a boy who grew up in such a positive home environment. I was also acutely aware that the education system appreciated very little of my own background and the associated struggles."

Mike became a Christian in 1982 at the age of fourteen after realising that unless God broke into his life, he was on a downward spiral. He went on to university to study urban studies, a subject that really lit his fire. He began to find answers to some of his questions like, "Why are urban communities so disadvantaged? What are the causes that underpin this inequality? What could be done to bring about real change?"

Mike's ongoing dedication to church-based youth work soon led to him being asked to pastor a church shortly after getting married to Viviene in his early twenties. The church was in West Yorkshire and that's where the Bradford connection began.

In the early days he worked with a number of churches on some youth projects, one of which, the Bradford New Life Church, had a community outreach called The Lighthouse. Mike was a pastor in a nearby town, but worked closely with them. In 1998 the organisation had grown to the point where charitable status became necessary and he became one of its founding trustees. The focus of the work began to sharpen and address the pressing need of many local young people whose lives were in education crisis.

Over the next five years, TLG developed an alternative education programme that offered the education department and local schools a programme with consistency and educational rigour, delivered by qualified staff with years of experience in working with disadvantaged young people.

By 2004 the vision to expand the work to other cities was born and TLG is now a national Christian charity working with young people aged eleven to sixteen who have been excluded from school or are in crisis in their education. It's a shock to realise that each year in the UK around 10,000 young people are permanently excluded from school with many more experiencing temporary exclusion. TLG aims to ensure young people aren't hindered by their past, but given a second chance of success.

As an alternative education provider, TLG aims to tackle the issues that cause behavioural difficulties for young people at risk of exclusion from school. The desire is to enable those children to raise their aspirations through innovative programmes that develop basic vocational and key skills.

"In the long term," Mike explains, "we want to see those young people re-integrated back into mainstream school while continuing to give them relational support. Ultimately, TLG wants to see the transformation of the lives of young people at every level – educationally, emotionally, behaviourally, socially and, of course, spiritually. When a young person is referred to us from the education department or a local school, our aim is to get 'buy in' from parents, carers, teachers, social workers and most importantly the young person themselves. Establishing the boundaries and offering an individual programme tailored to meet the specific needs of each young person is a key part of our success. The learning environment is also important. Young people work in groups of no more than eight with up to three staff. The informal nature of the physical space is the perfect antidote to young people who have struggled with mainstream school. We usually work with a young person for one or two terms, engaging them during school time, but also through extended school activities which run in partnership with a local church. It's during the beyond-school activities that the real transformation takes place, young people being willing to open up about their issues through an informal programme of activities that they have chosen to engage with. Every centre works slightly differently, depending on the local context. But the stories have an underlying theme: a restoration of hope and a positive outlook on the future for the young people we have engaged."

Ayasha's story

Ayasha began attending TLG three days a week after she started having problems at school: "I didn't used to like school, I used to skive a lot and started hanging around with the wrong people. I never listened and never did as I was told. I had no respect for anyone and in the end I couldn't be bothered." Ayasha's life changed dramatically while at TLG, which saw her going back into mainstream school permanently. "I've changed loads since being at TLG. It's a lot different from school. They explain stuff better and speak to you in a different way when you can't do things. I don't get bored in class now and I understand what I have to do. My attitude has got a lot better, the way I speak to people is different and I have more respect now. I've learnt loads since I've been here and I enjoy doing work now, I think it's fantastic."

Antony's Mum

Antony began attending TLG when he was expelled from school after failing to transfer his happy family life to school. "Before TLG came along he was constantly getting into trouble at school," she says, "and we were always getting phone calls to come and pick him up because he was kicking off and getting in fights all the time. This went on for a good eighteen months and the school just couldn't cope. We were at the point of being distraught, not knowing what to do. It was a total distraction for all the family." Antony's Mum's conclusion was, "TLG really put us at ease and made us appreciate that we weren't the only parents with a problem and that we weren't on our own. They where brilliant! Absolutely brilliant! They get results. You can see the difference in him now. He's currently doing further training to try and join the Police force."

TLG works in partnership with a number of organisations, formally and informally. In any city they work closely with the local education department and local schools as well a host of other statutory and voluntary providers. However, as Mike explains, "For us, the most important partnership is with the local church. Bill Hybels once said, 'the local church is the hope of the world.' TLG will only work in a new city in partnership with a local church. When you work with local church you are joining in with what God is already doing in a locality rather than parachuting in. There is often the opportunity to improve an underutilised church hall and maximise its benefit both for church and community. Most importantly, there is a welcoming family with which the young people we work with can find a sense of belonging and shared identity. While TLG is happy to take the lead on interventions for young people during school hours, we see our role as essentially empowering the local church to do the same beyond school hours. And to know that the church will be praying for the centre is priceless. The days of everyone working in their own bomb shelters are over. We can achieve so much more together."

"Our vision is to see a TLG centre serving young people in every city in the UK. We recognise that the issue of exclusion and educational crisis for young people will not go away. We are busy influencing policy formulation at a political level. However, replicating good practice across the country seems the best way to earn the right to speak about this issue. Our first new centre in Birmingham has been a great success and a real learning curve for the organisation. We are progressing partnerships for centres in London, Manchester, Nottingham and other cities. It's all about getting the right people on board the bus and then getting the right people in the right seats. Our mandate is to see the inclusive message of the Gospel touch the lives of the excluded. Our mandate is education, education, education and the transformation of every young person we have the opportunity to engage with."

Isn't it exciting hearing about all these dedicated people across our nation who have answered the call of God and are meeting head-on the challenges of our society in the name of Jesus? Like the mustard seed, these expressions of God's kingdom begin in relative obscurity, making only the smallest difference in one or two lives. As the seed germinates and sprouts, nurtured and watered by specific, focused prayer and radical, fearless unity, so the tiny plant becomes a tree and begins to provide shelter for large numbers of broken people. Like the yeast, the uplifting ministry of these Spirit-filled, Jesus-centred organisations permeates every area of the communities in which they work. The love and power of God reaches the people who most need it and brings redemption and transformation. Broken lives are repaired. Prisoners set free. Hallelujah!

Notes

1. www.capuk.org
2. www.thelighthousegroup.co.uk
3. John Kirkby, *Nevertheless*, published by Christians Against Poverty, first published 2003, 2nd edition 2006.

Beacons of Hope

Standing tall

The inevitable has happened, as I always knew it would. I have become the smallest person in my household. Our youngest child, Matthew, now stands an inch taller than the one who brought him into this world just fourteen years ago.

Not that I'm really bothered, in fact, quite the opposite – I'd be worried if my kids didn't outgrow their mum. As Pete Greig points out in his foreword, I'm not the tallest person in the world! In the same way, I'm always thrilled to see young people growing spiritually, even to the point where they seem to have more passion for God and His kingdom than their elders. It used to worry me slightly when I heard young people talk with enormous enthusiasm about their spiritual aspirations rather than making careful plans to build a career. Nowadays I take a more relaxed view: young people in the West have so much choice; let them put their career plans on hold for a while by all means if it means they're going to give themselves to the mission of making Christ known in word and deed at home and abroad.

Our son, Josh, who is eighteen, is currently training with The Message to be a schools evangelist. It's really exciting to see him revelling in his new world: learning about the Bible,

writing songs, doing lessons and assemblies in schools – none
of which was ever offered by his Careers Advisors at school!
He knows he can always go to university in a few years if he
wants to, or train for some other profession or trade. Right
now he's simply pouring out his life for the Gospel and that
makes me proud.

Frank and I recently visited Bolivia to observe the amazing
child sponsorship work of Compassion.[1] Travelling with us
was Roy Crowne (Youth For Christ[2] National Director) and
his twenty-one year old son, John, who was easily the star of
the whole team wherever we went. He managed to communicate with the children despite the language barrier and
didn't seem at all bothered by the lack of home comforts. We
found out to our shame that, while this was our first visit to a
developing country, John had done trips like this before. It
was so encouraging to see this young man building huge
learning principles into his experience of life rather than just
chasing the dream of material wealth as so many do at that
age. John has just completed his apprenticeship as a heating
engineer and is about to set up his own business (which is
another way of saying "I'm unemployed at the moment"!),
but that didn't stop him signing up to sponsor a little Bolivian
child.

When I think about the younger generation outgrowing us
I get so excited. I love young people; my own church is full of
them with our average age at twenty-something and getting
younger by the day. Young people are the hope for our
nation. We see in them massive potential and it is our job to
ensure they get all the help and love they need to get there.
People like Lucy Smith and her husband Andy are beacons of
hope in one of the toughest estates in Manchester. Their
home is open to the young people throughout the week; it's
not just about church on Sunday. Their given-away lives shine
brightly with the light of Jesus against the backdrop of
darkness that surrounds life on the margins. As a mature

adult whose children have grown up, if God called me, I might just about manage to move in and live long term in a tough inner-city estate. I could never have done so as a young person.

There are hundreds of young disciples who have said, "Whatever it takes Lord." A couple of years ago I was in Madrid speaking at the leaders' gathering of Contra Corriente,[3] a radical movement of young people from across Spain, and meeting some amazing, vibrant young people who are determined to influence Spain for Christ. I got into conversation with a young girl, the daughter of American pastors, who had been brought up in Spain. I asked her what she did and she replied that she was the leader of the 24-7 prayer movement. "In Madrid?" I asked, "No, in Spain," she replied without a flicker of either pride or false humility. That nation is in good hands!

This chapter features shining examples of young people who are doing great things for God and living out His prophetic word. Some of these stories feature young people who have been pioneering transformation for many years and others have been more recently inspired by the opportunities Hope08 will bring.

Hope08: Hope Revolution

Recently, Gavin Calver, Director of Church Resource for Youth For Christ , was interviewed by *Youthwork Magazine*[4] about young people and their involvement in Hope08.[5] Youth For Christ passionately believe in taking the good news relevantly to every young person in Britain and Hope08 presents an amazing opportunity for young people to shine. By the way, for those too young to remember, this is another example of a young man potentially outgrowing his parents: Gavin's father, Clive, was National Director of YFC many years ago! Here's an extract of the interview:

"How is Hope Revolution different from Hope08?"

"Hope Revolution[6] is the youth arm of Hope08. In many ways it's the dangerous form of Hope08. Throughout history, virtually all revolutions, both sacred and secular have been spearheaded by young people. Brave young people who are prepared to put their backs on the line for a cause they believe in. So it's an integral part of Hope08 – the vision is for the whole Church, adults and young people, to be effective in mission. Statistics say that 70% of western Christians come to faith before the age of 21 and 85% before the age of 23, and then Hope08's first place is in youth communities. So we've taken the adult collaboration and are inviting people under 19 to sign up asking God to 'change me, change my friends, change my community and change my world'."

"How are you hoping young people will get involved?"

"We're giving young people the opportunity to sign up or text HOPE 83010 and make a declaration of heart and intent to change something next year. But then what actually happens is up to the individuals. The idea is that they join with others to change things locally. The British Church Consensus claims that 742,000 young people have contact with a church every week, so we want to see 100,000 young people trying to change Britain next year. So we have a Facebook page,[7] a Myspace page[8] and a Hope Revolution website[9] for these individuals to know that they are part of something bigger, a revolution."

"What have you seen of this vision so far?"

"We're seeing young people freed up to dream big dreams. We know that Jeremiah was 17 and the disciples were no more than 22 or 23, and we're coming back to a time when the Church is recognising that young people can make a huge difference. We're telling people in a cynical world that 'you are old enough to be that city on a hill and a shining light.

You can be part of this revolution.' I was in Cardiff a short time ago at a Hope Revolution meeting where we were calling people to become revolutionaries. After the meeting, two lads of 16 asked if they could pray with me for God to help them to live in this way. One of the lads asked for God to help him change his school, and the when the other lad prayed for him, he asked him to forgive his friend for having too small a vision and instead said, 'help him to believe he can change his community'! I was challenged by that. It reminded me that we all need that youthful enthusiasm and expectation that something can change and we can be part of seeing that. After another conference, we saw young people praying for revival for an hour, so we had to delay the after-hours entertainment. So we're seeing a generation who are being freed to have big expectations."

"And what resources and help are being provided to support this vision?"
"There is material at our website: ideas, a theme of the week and thoughts alongside the 'Change me, change my friends etc.' tagline. Hope08 are really providing a skeleton framework of ideas for groups to take on and develop."

"If youth groups and churches are already trying to do work in their communities, what difference will Hope Revolution make?"
"This is not a new project, but the one unique selling point to this whole vision is unity. We will be doing this together at the same time. We're hoping that this can be a catalyst for change in Kent, Manchester, Nottingham, wherever. We're using the excuse of Hope08 to encourage and empower tens of thousands of young people to work locally where they are. We're not taking them all away into just the city this time, but encouraging them to see mission where they are. But the unique selling point is that everyone is together . . ."

"What would be the success of Hope Revolution?"

"I'd love to see in ten years time there being no need for 'how to do marketplace ministry', because people learnt to do it at school. If teenagers learn to make mission and service the fabric of their lives, we'll see a generation grow who do this throughout their lives. For adults, Hope08 provides an exciting opportunity in the midst of their lives to do something different, but for teenagers, we can inspire them during these formative years. Then it can change their culture, change the way they hold themselves and we'll see the outworking of that way beyond 2008."[10]

Ignite Hope: Cardiff

A group of young people in Dinas Powys, Wales, were inspired by their experience at Soul in the City in London, 2004. Here John Lewis tells us how the encouragement of seeing Soul in the City working inspired them to take on Dinas Powys and the city of Cardiff:

"In 2004, about twenty young people from two churches in Dinas Powys (Bethesda Chapel and Dinas Powys Baptist church) went to London to take part in Soul in the City,[11] something which most of us had never experienced before. We didn't really know what to expect, as we had never done this 'social action' thing before. A few weeks before we went I broke my leg, which wasn't good, so I didn't know what I was going to do in a wheelchair for the whole thing!

The whole Soul in the City experience was awesome, for all of us. This was something completely new, going out into the community to clear someone's garden. Walking around estates picking up litter which wasn't yours. People were walking past us, wondering why we were picking up litter for free, and asking us, 'Why are you doing this?' It started to hit me how much of an impact we were making in the community, people just couldn't understand why we were doing all of this for free!

Coming back from London was a huge anticlimax, back to 'same old' Dinas Powys. All of us were just on fire and couldn't settle for going back to where we live and doing nothing!

Two of us were in a car a couple of days after, praying on a hill. We were ready to take on Cardiff! We started coming up with ideas of doing what we did in London, back here in Dinas Powys, our local village. We decided to do 'Soul in Dinas'.[12] A group of us started to meet every Wednesday to pray about this project, as none of us knew what action to take other than commit it to God. Planning started to take shape and we came up with a date of running a summer week at the end of August. None of us had much experience of organising this type of project, but God led the way. The vision of Soul in Dinas is the 'whole church and whole community'. We knew that unity was so important which led us to try and get all the churches in Dinas Powys involved as much as possible. As it came to the summer week 2005, we had over 100 volunteers from churches over Dinas Powys which was incredible. We delivered a leaflet to every house in Dinas Powys which explained all the stuff we had planned with a tear-off slip so that people could send it back to us with the jobs they wanted to be done! This worked really well, people sent their slips back, some jobs were only small, and some jobs were huge. But we were up for it!

We met every morning during Soul in Dinas week for worship and prayer, then moved out to the community as one army for Jesus! After the day we came back for an evening meal and held BBQs in the evening with a music youth event. The week was crazy, so much amazing stuff going on, that it was hard to keep track of it all. I think we all started to realise the seeds that were being sown in the community.

One project we did was clearing a huge overgrown area at

the side of a pub. It had been overgrown for years, local residents were not happy with it, and nothing was really being done about it. We decided to hack our way into the brambles and get it looking like it should! The owner of the pub saw what we were doing and told us to stop because he was going to get someone else to do it! We refused to move! So, he started bringing pints of coke out for all of the volunteers as everyone was boiling! He kept on asking why we were doing it and he was saying how he would pay for someone to come and do this! He couldn't understand why we were doing it for free. Even though it has a huge task, the result was incredible. People walking by were amazed at the difference! Quite often, residents would stop on the corner and just stare at us! One woman stopped on the corner for about half hour telling everyone that walked past what we were doing! Being in the community doing this was quite a strange experience for some, as we are so used to being inside the walls of the church, with the doors closed. To do this was quite radical. We realised that when we make ourselves available and ready for God, He moves in and uses us for His kingdom!

The first 'Soul in Dinas' was awesome so we thought, let's do it again! We continued to meet every Wednesday to plan for the next one in 2006! Seeing the unity between the churches throughout the week was something which really stuck out. Even though we believed different things, we all knew that Jesus was the centre of it all, and that is what unites us.

The next Soul in Dinas had, again, over one hundred volunteers. All of us gathered together for five days to go and show the community who Jesus is! By now, people knew us; they felt they could approach us instead of being separate. People who had no connection with church, would not walk through the church doors, were able to approach us. We were available to go to them and meet them where they are, just as Jesus would do.

We were all so excited, we didn't really know what was going to happen next, we were just ready and willing to do what God wanted in Dinas Powys.

Three of us were talking after a service one Sunday night when one of the guys who took part in Soul In Dinas shared something with us. It was the vision of Dinas Powys and surrounding areas being a dry forest. A spark was ignited and before you knew it the whole forest was blazing. Amazingly this was the same picture that another leader was given a year ago from someone at an event in Cardiff. We were all so excited about this, we didn't know what to do next!

About a month later we came together again to pray for guidance with the next step. We realised that a lot of us had big stuff on in the coming year: A Levels, a degree to finish, and marriage! So we were all wondering how it would end up! In December 2006 a few people in group felt God was saying to lay the project down and wait on Him, for this is not 'our' project, it is His.

In July 2007, Nathan and I met up with Gary Smith, one of the leaders of Ignite[13] (a youth organisation based in Cardiff). He talked to both of us about a project that he was thinking of doing as part of Hope 2008. The idea was to run a four day mission, just like Soul in the City, but here in Cardiff, South Wales! Gary asked us what we were doing next year. At this time we were both going travelling! Soon enough, plans changed and we were both on board to work full time for this project. Gary asked us because of our experience with planning Soul in Dinas. Even though it was a small project it was definitely training ground for both of us to take on this massive project.

So this is where we are now, planning for this big mission 'IgniteHope'[14] from 2–5 May, 2008. There is so much amazing stuff going on all over the UK this year under the Hope08 banner. Also alongside IgniteHope, we are going to be heading up a year of Hope in Dinas Powys. Soul In Dinas will be a big part of this, as we plan for the next summer week in 2008.

Be encouraged that when we make ourselves available to God, He steps in and uses us for His glory. We want to see God change this nation, so let's pray that we will be a generation that rises up for God, that serves Him with *all* of our hearts. Amen."

Eden, Harpurhey

Eden[15] is an award-winning and influential approach to urban youth work and community transformation. Eden recognises that young people's lives are tangled with all sorts of relationships, aspirations and frustrations. Working with them successfully requires a holistic, long term approach embracing their family, their education, their health and, of course, their relationship with God.[16]

The unique thing about Eden is the choice made by numbers of young adults to live in the most difficult areas, sharing the problems of those growing up there and ministering to their needs. Many who choose to move into an Eden area are also choosing to move out of a comfortable life and out of a promising career at a time when conventional wisdom says one ought to be laying strong foundations for future promotion.

Every community they work in has different challenges, but one thing is true in all the areas: they really need stability. By making homes in the area long term Eden teams have shown that even the most volatile neighbourhoods can be tamed.

> *"Forget the former things;*
> *do not dwell on the past.*
> *See, I am doing a new thing!*
> *Now it springs up, do you not perceive it?*

I am making a way in the desert
   and streams in the wasteland
The wild animals will honour me,
   the jackals and the owls,
because I provide water in the desert
   and streams in the wasteland,
to give drink to my people, my chosen,
   the people I formed myself
   that they may proclaim praise."

                                        (Isaiah 43:18–21)

This is the foundational scripture for the nine Eden projects around Manchester and provides great encouragement to people like Lucy Smith, who is part of the Eden project in Harpuhey. Lucy writes:

"Our project started in 2001 with a team of fifteen (now slightly smaller) run by a young evangelist, Ian Henderson. I joined three years later in 2004. For our team, we hold on strongly to this passage from Isaiah 43. We are determined not to look at the past, at how this deprived area has been seen, and we press on with the hope and knowledge that God is doing a new thing. In a 2004 Government survey, Harpurhey was proclaimed as being the worst place to live in the UK. It was said to have the worst rate of social and economic deprivation in the nation at that time.

At the start of the project the aim was initially to get to know the area and the young people. The team would spend a lot of time prayer walking, worshipping, praying and getting to know the young people through trips and home groups. During the first few years some of the young people wanted to push the boundaries to see how long we'd stay, and whether our concern for them was genuine. There are numerous stories of front doors being covered with dog poo, bricks through windows and general verbal abuse. Some of the incidents were very serious, including one of our team members being covered in petrol and a young person trying to set them alight. There was a real physical battle.

One of the ways God started to speak to us about how the 'wild animals' would one day honour Jesus (Isaiah 43), was through the power of worship as a weapon of warfare. He started to show us how He wanted to use worship, especially through music, to break down strongholds and bring breakthrough. Jess Davis, a member of our team, brought a prophecy from 2 Chronicles 17–22, where God tells Jehoshaphat not to fight but to worship, and God wins the battle for them. At this time we were holding an Eden team worship night at a church where we had our office. However, we were really struggling with local people coming in and disturbing our meetings. On one occasion some young lads came in with balaclavas and toy guns. As God continued to speak to us about worship and warfare we realised the importance of moving the worship night to the actual church we were serving and really interceding there. Since then, we have rarely had to police the services in the same way, and the physical violence started to dwindle for the team in Harpurhey.

At Easter time, 2007, the church down the road, Harpurhey Community Church, had a Maundy Thursday meal and invited us to go. A good number of us made it down and together we had a powerful time of reflection on Jesus' journey to the cross. On the Saturday night of the Easter weekend a few of us got together in our prayer room to see the Easter morning in through prayer and praise. The next morning we had such a great celebration at church, the Lord was really present and there was lots of joy.

At the end of the service our vicar, Canon Mark Ashcroft, said, 'We have a surprise for you...' Then the pastor from Harpurhey Community Church walked down the aisle, took the microphone and began to explain that they were so thankful that we went to see them on Thursday night that they finished their church service early, their whole church walked to our church and were waiting outside to celebrate with us and bless us with their tea, coffee, hot cross buns and muffins! There was a standing ovation as about one hundred and twenty people walked down the aisle and congregated at the top of church. People were standing on the pews whistling and cheering, and there were a few tears shed. As we all stood worshipping the risen Jesus I suddenly realised that this is what we had been waiting for, and how beautiful it was. Canon Mark Ashcroft recalls, 'It was an amazing time of joy together and a powerful confirmation of what the Lord had been saying to us as a church about the importance of unity, that God's power and presence will be fully revealed when we local churches do things together. We were all blown away by the love and generosity of our sister church. What an amazing God we worship!'

A few Sundays after Easter we were continuing our sermon series at church on 'God is love' and we were focusing on the thought that it is greater to give than to receive. We felt the Lord speaking to us about blessing the Police. In this estate the Police don't have a particularly good reputation, so this was an extreme challenge for many. We were led in a time of repentance for all the things that our community has called the Police, and then we wanted to do something practical for them.

We decided on taking a collection, enough for a box of chocolates (we hoped), and to write a page of 'thank you' notes. To our amazement, the collection was way beyond what we expected and we filled three A4 pages with thank you's! During the following week we took a group of the young people and went to the local Police Station to deliver the gifts, our blessings, and tell them of how it all came about. Again, we were amazed by what God did. The police officers were blown away. They kept saying things like, 'In all my years of service I have never seen anyone thanks us like this.' It was a real privilege.

Our heart is to be a community that loves instead of hates, a community where the young people who were the problem become the answer, a community where there is freedom rather than addiction, a community where there are streams of living water flowing ... and a community where there is spiritual drought no more!

We are not there yet, but we're not where we used to be either, praise God! We have seen a steady flow of young people moving closer and closer to Christ. A solid core of newly-converted youngsters has emerged and we're working with them daily, helping them to grow and develop as disciples. We have a long way to go but we've also got plenty of time because we're not going away! We are believing for the revival God has promised."

XLP: Urban Youth Charity, London

Patrick Regan is the founder and leader of XLP,[17] a dedicated team working in inner-city schools and neighbourhoods in London and beyond. In 1996, in response to a stabbing in a school playground, the school's headmaster asked Patrick Regan, a local church-based youth worker, to come into the school and work with their students and teachers to help with difficult behavioural issues. This was the beginning of XLP, a Christian charity that has an emphasis on being faith-based, but not faith-biased – XLP works equally with young people of all faiths and those who have none. Those who work at XLP share a common passion: to serve the community by meeting the social, educational and behavioural needs of young people, and empowering them to make wise lifestyle choices and to realise their potential.

One of the most recent projects, Gunzdown,[18] has been focused on guns and knives in schools and issues such as identity and anger management. Teamed with one of the UK's leading hip-hop bands, Greenjade, XLP have been touring the schools performing an hour-long multi-media event combined with follow-up lessons dealing with these issues.

In July 2003, XLP was awarded the inaugural Queen's Golden Jubilee Award for voluntary service by groups in the community. The award was granted in recognition of XLP "working with and supporting schools, families and communities in South London".

In his book, *Conspiracy of the Insignificant*,[19] Patrick recounts the story of one youngster called Jason when asked describe the experience of coming to XLP lunch clubs:

"I was always in trouble at school, always in fights. It wasn't about winning fights – I rarely started them – but about surviving and getting through another day. My mum kicked me out when I was five, so I went to live with my dad and my stepmother. I don't see my mum. I don't even know where she is and she never contacts me.

My friends and I started going to the XLP lunch club, Extreme, and I enjoyed playing the games and having a laugh with my mates. After a while I started listening more to the things Patrick and the team were saying about God, and they started to make more sense to me. I made friends with the XLP team and thought they were all really cool and were always interested in me and what was going on in my life.

When they started doing an after-school club I went along and that was where I gave my life to God. As I prayed I felt my spine begin to tingle and ever since my heart's been on fire for God. Even in the winter I don't feel the cold and people are always asking why I don't wear a coat even when it's snowing. It's God's Spirit that keeps me warm now.

Before I started doing the XLP lunch club I was on the verge of being kicked out of school for always having fights, but the more I got to know about God, the less I seemed to get in trouble. Going to the lunch club gave me something to belong to and it boosted my self-confidence. I didn't have many friends before so it really meant something to me to have somewhere to be, and I couldn't believe it when I realised Jesus was not only my Saviour but also the best friend I could ever have. My teachers can't believe how much I've improved and I even got one of the highest marks in our end-of-term tests which would never have happened before.

I've stayed out of trouble for a while now. People still try and wind me up because I used to be an easy target, but now I just calm myself down and while I don't let them walk all over me, I don't use my fists any more. My bedroom has marks in the wall where I would punch it when I was really angry. When I see them it just reminds me of how far I've come.

I've started playing guitar and writing songs to God because I just want to worship Him and tell people what He's done for me. Recently I gave my testimony at church and one of my mates came along and when he heard it he became a Christian too – it was the best feeling. When I leave school I'd love to do the XLP year-out eXperience and then maybe go on to be a youth worker so I can help other people who feel as isolated as I did, because what XLP have done for me has completely changed my life."[20]

FireStarters: Glasgow

FireStarters[21] began in 1996 with a vision to see young people in Scotland knowing their God-given identity and being able to make a difference in the world around them. FireStarters have been running monthly "mission weekends" with around one hundred young people since its launch in 1996, partnering with churches across the central belt of Scotland. In September 2006, energies were focused in the East End of Glasgow. The aims of FireStarters are to equip and mobilise teenagers to love God and to serve in practical ways to make His love known to others. Since moving the focus to East

Glasgow, more specific local area needs and opportunities have evolved.

The impact on local communities and churches which the young people are serving has predominantly been that of building trust. Many denominations are working together alongside FireStarters enabling outreach programmes to happen. Teams in the East End are now running children's clubs, youth cafés, prayer walking, a monthly youth event and community and garden clear-ups. There is a new exciting partnership with a church in Dalmarnock which is where the Commonwealth Games stadium will be built. It is a poor area, but they have had some wonderful initial connections with the community and will work with them towards preparing for the games in 2014.

As a result of the FireStarters project, young people have found freedom through prayer from controlling eating disorders and self-harm, and have received physical and emotional healing.

Young people in big urban cities are responding to the challenge of the Gospel to reach out to hurting communities and win a lost generation for Christ. Young people in the rural communities are also sensing a need to respond to the call of God. God loves communities and so do they.

Love Cornwall

In May 2006 a group of Christian leaders were praying at the Christian Resources Exhibition[22] in Surrey. They felt that it was right to pour their resources and their energy into one county, to spark off a mission that might draw churches together in a bid to see their communities transformed and touched by God's love and power.

After more prayer and thought, Cornwall came to mind. That group summoned David Hull, a Methodist minister in Par (a town near St Austell on the south coast) to a meeting the next day. In that time it became clear that Cornwall was ripe and ready for something new. Cornwall has a history of revival that dates back to the Wesleys.

David Hull took the vision of that group to a group of thirty ecumenical church leaders in Cornwall and "Love Cornwall 06"[23] was born. The mission was planned for a month in July 2006. During that time, churches caught the vision and began to plan together.

Love Cornwall 06, which included a few bigger events in the Royal Cornwall Showground such as free cream teas, youth events and gigs, was a massive encouragement. It was encouraging that together, something could be done for the kingdom in partnership. The churches in Liskeard began a partnership that endures to this day. But David Hull and the executive of LoveCornwall 06 felt that more could be done with greater planning.

Love Cornwall 08 has all the same aims as the 2006 mission. This time, however, the vision has been given a higher profile in Cornwall through Hope08. As part of the 2008 mission, a youth exchange programme idea emerged, where youth groups could request a few young people to get alongside their own youth group to do something sustainable in their area. That could mean getting out on the streets and praying for people, or it could mean inviting their friends round for pizza and having someone share their testimony. The hope is that the youth exchange will encourage young people who are often the only sub-eighty year olds in their church that there are other youth who love Jesus out there, and provide a framework for future outreach in host churches.

The organisers write, "2008 will see 500 young people together over the bank holiday weekend in May, camping at a holiday resort in Perranporth (the campsite felt that they wanted to give us a 65% discount on accommodation). Friday night will be a night of worship, teaching, equipping and ministry. Then on the Saturday and Sunday, groups of eighty young people will be bussed out to towns around Cornwall to do social action projects and street evangelism. We have bands booked to put on events in each town which people can be invited to. The hope is that we will fill venues and proclaim the Gospel to hundreds of people around the county. The vision is not just to form relationships and give the God a good press through serving, but to make Him clearly known to the people of each town. Cornwall Prayer Initiative[24] has been praying for the young people of Cornwall for years. And we know that we are starting to see breakthrough."

Greater things

When Jesus said, "You will do greater things than these," it was a prophetic statement. It was not primarily foretelling, but forth telling. The prophetic word is creative, not merely predictive. The nature of the prophetic word when God speaks it is to call things into being rather than predicting what will be. His word challenges things to come to pass.

When He said, "You will do greater things," it was more of a command than a prediction. He was saying, "You better had do greater things," and with "You have it in you to do greater things," He speaks to the potential. We need to speak in a similar vein to our young people – speak to their potential, call out from within them the latent excellence and godly passion. We can't afford to be embarrassed about them outgrowing us or over-concerned about the merely natural aspects of their personal development. We should rejoice at their willingness to seek first the kingdom of God and direct their energies to its advancement.

*Notes*_____

1. www.compassionuk.org
2. www.yfc.co.uk
3. www.contracorriente.org

4. www.youthwork.co.uk
5. www.hope08.com
6. www.hope-revolution.com
7. www.facebook.com/group.php?gid=2248168938
8. www.myspace.com/thehoperevolution
9. www.hope-revolution.com
10. *Youth Work Magazine*, November 2007 issue.
11. www.soulinthecity.org.uk
12. www.soulindinas.co.uk
13. www.igniteme.org
14. www.thornhillyouth.com/ignitehope
15. www.message.org.uk/edenproject.cfm
16. Matt Wilson, *Eden: Called to the Streets* (Kingsway Publications, 2005, ISBN: 978-1-842912-19-5).
17. www.xlp.org.uk
18. www.xlp.org.uk/community/GunzDown
19. Patrick Regan and Liza Hoeksma *Conspiracy of the Insignificant* (Survivor, 2007).
20. Regan, *Conspiracy* (Survivor, 2007), pp. 152–153. Extract used by permission.
21. www.firestartersuk.co.uk
22. www.creonline.co.uk
23. www.cosmiccomputers.co.uk/love_cornwall/index.html
24. www.transform-cornwall.co.uk

Get in Touch with Redeeming Our Communities

See our website:

www.redeemingourcommunities.org.uk

for the latest news from around the UK, information about events and conferences, more resources to inspire you, and forums to discuss your own projects.

You can also sign up to receive our monthly news bulletin and order our latest DVDs.

ROC is a City Links initiative:
www.citylinks.org.uk

Redeeming Our Communities
City Links
Lancaster House
Harper Road, Sharston
Manchester M22 4RG

About the Author

Debra Green is the Director of City Links, an organisation that seeks to promote partnerships for spiritual and social transformation through prayer and action. Debra is also on the pastoral staff team of Ivy Cottage Church, Didsbury.

She is a pioneer of prayer and prophetic ministries and has travelled widely in the UK and abroad teaching about prayer and outreach for cities. She provides consultancy on citywide prayer and networking strategies which help to transform communities and make mission more effective. She is a regular speaker at Christian conferences.

Debra is the author of *City-Changing Prayer* (Survivor) co-authored with her husband, Frank, and *Redeeming Our Communities* (New Wine Press).

We hope you enjoyed reading this New Wine book.
For details of other New Wine books
and a range of 2,000 titles from other
Word and Spirit publishers visit our website:
www.newwineministries.co.uk
email: newwine@xalt.co.uk